101 Crochet Squares™

each color. Take the average yardage, and multiply it by the number of squares to be made. To this, add sufficient yardage for assembling, any edgings and fringe that you might want to make.

Introduction
Unlike most crochet patterns, those in this book specify no gauge—and no suggested hook size and no yarn amounts!

That's because each square can be worked with your choice of yarn—from bulky to crochet cotton—to achieve just the look you want. Refer to the color photographs of all 101 squares to inspire you.

Size
In this book, the squares shown were all worked with worsted weight yarn to a gauge of 4 dc and 2 dc rows = 1".

You may wish to experiment with a variety of yarns and hook sizes until you achieve the look that pleases you.

How much yarn will you need?
To determine how much yarn you will need for a project, whether it is an afghan, a sweater, a hat or a baby jacket, first make up three squares, using the actual yarn and hook size you will use for the project, being sure to leave at least 3" of yarn to weave in later with every color change. Carefully rip out the three squares, and measure the yardage of yarn used for

About color...
Many of the squares use more than one color. We have specified what colors we used to make the samples, but you are free to change the colors as you wish.

Many of the one-color squares could be worked in two or more colors; many of the multicolored squares would be equally pretty in one color. ●

Square 1

Materials
- Yarn—Color A light gold; Color B dark purple; Color C light purple; Color D off white

Instructions

Pansy
With Color A, ch 2.

Rnd 1 (RS): 5 sc in 2nd ch from hook; join in first sc. Change to Color B by drawing lp through; cut Color A.

Rnd 2: Ch 1, sc in same sc; [ch 6, 2 sc in next sc] 4 times; ch 6, sc in same sc as first sc made—*5 ch-6 sps*. Change to Color C by drawing lp through; do not finish off Color B.

Rnd 3: *Sl st in next ch-6 sp, in same sp work (sc, hdc, dc, ch 1, [tr, ch 1] 10 times; dc, hdc, sc)—*large petal made*; rep from * once more; **sl st in next ch-6 sp, in same sp work (sc, hdc, 8 dc, hdc, sc)—*small petal made*; rep from ** twice more; join in first sl st—*2 large petals and 3 small petals*. Change to Color B by drawing lp through; cut Color C.

Rnd 4: *Sc in next sc, in next hdc, in next dc, and in next ch-1 sp; [ch 3, sc in next ch-1 sp] 10 times; sc in next dc, in next hdc, and in next sc; sl st in next sl st; rep from * once more; [sc in next 12 sts, sl st in next sl st] twice; sc in next 12 sts; join in joining sl st of prev rnd. Finish off Color B and weave in all ends.

Square
With Color D, ch 4; join to form a ring.

Rnd 1 (RS): Ch 1, 8 sc in ring; join in first sc.

Rnd 2: Ch 1, sc in same sc; ch 3, [sc in next sc, ch 3] 7 times; join in first sc—*8 ch-3 sps*.

Rnd 3: Sl st in next ch-3 sp, ch 1, sc in same sp; ch 3, [sc in next ch-3 sp, ch 3] 7 times; join in first sc.

Rnd 4: Ch 1, sc in same sc; ch 3, sc in next ch-3 sp, ch 3; *sc in next sc, ch 3, sc in next ch-3 sp, ch 3; rep from * 6 times more; join in first sc—*16 ch-3 sps*.

Rnd 5: Sl st in next ch-3 sp, ch 3 *(counts as a dc on this and following rnds)*, in same sp work (dc, ch 2, 2 dc)—*beg corner made*; *ch 3, [sc in next ch-3 sp, ch 3] 3 times; in next ch-3 sp work (2 dc, ch 2, 2 dc)—*corner made*; rep from * 3 times more, ending last rep without working last corner; join in 3rd ch of beg ch-3.

Rnd 6: Ch 3, dc in next dc; *in next corner ch-2 sp work corner; dc in next 2 dc, [sc in next ch-3 sp, ch 3] 3 times; sc in next ch-3 sp, dc in next 2 dc; rep from * 3 times more, ending last rep without working last 2 dc; join in 3rd ch of beg ch-3.

Rnd 7: Ch 3, dc in next 3 dc; *corner in next corner; dc in next 4 dc and in next sc, [sc in next ch-3 sp, ch 3] twice; sc in next ch-3 sp, dc in next sc and in next 4 dc; rep from * 3 times more, ending last rep without working last 4 dc; join in 3rd ch of beg ch-3.

Rnd 8: Ch 3, dc in next 5 dc; *corner in next corner; dc in next 7 dc and in next sc, keeping last lp of each tr on hook, tr in next 2 ch-3 sps, yo and draw through all 3 lps on hook—*cluster made*; dc in next sc and in next 7 dc; rep from * 3 times more, ending last rep without working last 6 dc; join in 3rd ch of beg ch-3. Finish off Color D.

Rnd 9: Join Color B in any corner ch-2 sp; ch 1, 3 sc in same sp—*sc corner made*; sc in next 21 sts; *3 sc in next corner ch-2 sp—*sc corner made*; sc in next 21 sts; rep from * twice more; join in first sc.

Finish off and weave in all ends.

Finishing
With tapestry needle, tack Pansy to center of Square. ●

Square 2

Materials
- Yarn—Color A yellow; Color B pink; Color C dark green; Color D off white

Pattern Stitches
Front Post Single Crochet (fpsc): Insert hook from front to back to front around post *(see page 98)* of st indicated, draw up lp, yo and draw through 2 lps on hook—*fpsc made.*

Double Triple Crochet (dtr): Yo 3 times, draw up lp in sp indicated, (yo and draw through 2 lps on hook) 4 times—*dtr made.*

Instructions
With Color A, ch 6; join to form a ring.

Rnd 1 (RS): Ch 3 *(counts as a dc on this and following rnds)*, 15 dc in ring; join in 3rd ch of beg ch-3—*16 dc.*

Rnd 2: Ch 1, sc in same ch; ch 5, [sk next dc, sc in next dc, ch 5] 7 times; join in first sc—*8 ch-5 sps.* Finish off Color A.

Rnd 3: Join Color B in any ch-5 sp; ch 3, in same sp work (6 dc, ch 3, sl st in 3rd ch from hook, 7 dc)—*beg petal made*; in each rem ch-5 sp work (7 dc, ch 3, sl st in 3rd ch from hook, 7 dc)—*petal made*; join in 3rd ch of beg ch-3—*8 petals.* Finish off Color B.

Rnd 4: With RS facing you and working behind petals made in prev rnd, join Color C around post *(see page 98)* of any sc on Rnd 2; ch 1, **fpsc** *(see Pattern Stitches)* around same post; ch 5, [fpsc around next sc, ch 5] 7 times; join in first fpsc—*8 ch-5 sps.*

Rnd 5: Sl st in next ch-5 sp, ch 3, 5 dc in same sp; 6 dc in each rem ch-5 sp; join in 3rd ch of beg ch-3—*48 dc.*

Rnd 6: Ch 3, in same ch work (dc, ch 1, 2 dc); sk next 2 dc; *in next dc work (2 dc, ch 1, 2 dc); sk next 2 dc; rep from * 14 times more; join in 3rd ch of beg ch-3.

Finish off Color C.

Rnd 7: Join Color D in any ch-1 sp; ch 5 *(counts as a dtr)*, in same sp work (2 tr, ch 3, 2 tr, **dtr**—*see Pattern Stitches*]—*beg corner made*; *4 dc in next ch-1 sp; 4 hdc in next ch-1 sp; 4 dc in next ch-1 sp; in next ch-1 sp work (dtr, 2 tr, ch 3, 2 tr, dtr)—*corner made*; rep from * 3 times more, ending last rep without working last corner; join in 5th ch of beg ch-5.

Rnd 8: Ch 1, sc in same ch and in next 2 sts, 5 sc in next corner ch-3 sp—*sc corner made*; *sc in next 18 sts, 5 sc in next corner ch-3 sp—*sc corner made*; rep from * twice more; sc in next 15 sts; join in first sc.

Finish off and weave in all ends. ●

Square 3

Materials
- Yarn—Color A dark red; Color B off white; Color C pink

Instructions

Heart
Starting at point of Heart with Color A, ch 2.

Row 1 (RS): 3 sc in 2nd ch from hook. Ch 1, turn.

Row 2: 2 sc in next sc; sc in next sc, 2 sc in next sc—*5 sc*. Ch 1, turn.

Row 3: 2 sc in next sc; sc in next 3 sc, 2 sc in next sc—*7 sc*. Ch 1, turn.

Row 4: 2 sc in next sc; sc in next 5 sc, 2 sc in next sc—*9 sc*. Ch 1, turn.

Row 5: Sc in each sc. Ch 1, turn.

Row 6: Rep Row 5.

Top of Heart

First Side
Row 1: Sc in next 4 sc, sl st in next sc. Ch 1, turn, leaving rem 4 sc unworked.

Row 2: Dec over next 2 sc (to work dec: draw up lp in each of next 2 sc, yo and draw through all 3 lps on hook—*dec made*); dec as before—*2 sc*. Ch 1, turn.

Row 3: Sc in each sc; sl st in side of next 2 rows, sl st in same sc on Row 6 as last sl st made.

Second Side
Row 1: Sc in next 4 sc. Ch 1, turn.

Row 2: Dec twice; sl st in same sc on Row 6 as last sl st made—*2 sc*. Ch 1, turn.

Row 3: Sc in each sc. Ch 1, do not turn.

Edging
Rnd 1: Sc in side of each of next 9 rows; 3 sc in unused lp of beg ch; sc in side of each of next 9 rows; join in back lp *(see page 98)* of first sc. Change to Color B by drawing lp through; cut Color A.

Rnd 2: Ch 3, working in back lps only, *sl st in next sc, ch 3; rep from * around; join in back lp of joining sl st of prev rnd.

Finish off and weave in all ends.

Square
With Color C, ch 5; join to form a ring.

Rnd 1 (RS): Ch 3 *(counts as a dc on this and following rnds)*, 11 dc in ring; join in 3rd ch of beg ch-3—*12 dc*.

Rnd 2: Ch 3, dc in same ch; 2 dc in each rem dc; join in 3rd ch of beg ch-3—*24 dc.*

Rnd 3: Ch 3, in same ch work (2 dc, ch 3, 3 dc)—*beg corner made;* *dc in next dc, hdc in next 3 dc, dc in next dc, in next dc work (3 dc, ch 3, 3 dc)—*corner made;* rep from * 3 times more, ending last rep without working last corner; join in 3rd ch of beg ch-3.

Rnd 4: Ch 3, 2 dc in same ch; *in next corner ch-3 sp work corner; [sk next 2 sts, 3 dc in next st] 3 times; rep from * 3 times more, ending last rep without working last 3 dc; join in 3rd ch of beg ch-3. Finish off Color C.

Rnd 5: Join Color B in any corner ch-3 sp; ch 1, 3 sc in same sp—*sc corner made;* *sc in next 15 dc, 3 sc in next corner ch-3 sp—*sc corner made;* rep from * 3 times more, ending last rep without working last corner; join in front lp of first sc.

Rnd 6: Ch 3, working in front lps only, *sl st in next sc, ch 3; rep from * around; join in joining sl st of prev rnd. Finish off Color B.

Rnd 7: Working behind ch-3 sps of Rnd 6 in unused lps of Rnd 5, join Color C in unused lp of 2nd sc of any corner on Rnd 5; ch 3, in same lp work (2 dc, ch 2, 3 dc)—*beg dc corner made;* dc in next 17 lps; *in next lp work (3 dc, ch 2, 3 dc)—*dc corner made;* dc in next 17 lps; rep from * twice more; join in 3rd ch of beg ch-3.

Finish off and weave in all ends.

Finishing

With tapestry needle, tack Heart to center of Square. ●

Square 4

Materials

- Yarn—Color A turquoise; Color B emerald green; Color C off white

Instructions

Flower

With Color A, ch 6; join to form a ring.

Rnd 1: Ch 3 *(counts as a dc on this and following rnds),* 3 dc in ring; ch 3, turn; dc in first dc, in next 2 dc and in 3rd ch of beg ch-3—*petal made;* ch 3, turn; *working across back of petal just made, 4 dc in ring; ch 3, turn; dc in first dc and in next 3 dc—*petal made;* ch 3, turn; rep from * 6 times more; join in 3rd ch of beg ch-3 of first petal—*8 petals.* Finish off Color A.

Hold flower with petals facing you; working behind petals, join Color B in any ch-3 sp.

Rnd 2 (RS): Ch 3, in same sp work (2 dc, ch 2, 3 dc)—*beg corner made;* 3 dc in next ch-3 sp; *in next ch-3 sp work (3 dc, ch 2, 3 dc)—*corner made;* 3 dc in next ch-3 sp; rep from * twice more; join in 3rd ch of beg ch-3. Finish off Color B.

Rnd 3: Join Color C in any corner ch-2 sp; beg corner in same sp; *[3 dc in sp between next two 3-dc groups] twice; in next corner ch-2 sp work corner; rep from * twice more; [3 dc in sp between next two 3-dc groups] twice; join in 3rd ch of beg ch-3.

Rnd 4: Ch 1, sc in same ch and in next 2 dc; *3 sc in next corner ch-3 sp—*sc corner made*; sc in next 12 dc; rep from * twice more; 3 sc in next corner ch-3 sp—*sc corner made*; sc in next 9 dc; join in first sc.

Finish off and weave in all ends. ●

Square 5

Materials

- Yarn—Color A light gold; Color B emerald green; Color C off white

Instructions

Flower

With Color A, ch 2.

Rnd 1 (RS): 6 sc in 2nd ch from hook; join in first sc.

First Petal

Row 1: Ch 1, 2 sc in same sc. Ch 1, turn.

Row 2: 2 sc in each sc—*4 sc*. Ch 1, turn.

Row 3: 2 sc in next sc; sc in next 2 sc, 2 sc in next sc—*6 sc*. Ch 1, turn.

Row 4: Sc in each sc. Ch 1, turn.

Row 5: Dec over next 2 sc (to work dec: draw up lp in each of next 2 sc, yo and draw through all 3 lps on hook—*dec made*); sc in next 2 sc, dec as before—*4 sc*. Ch 1, turn.

Row 6: Dec twice—*2 sc*. Ch 3, turn.

Row 7: Sk next sc, sl st in next sc and in side of each of next 6 rows of petal; sl st in last sc worked on Row 1 and in next sc. Do not turn. Do not finish off.

2nd Petal

Row 1: Ch 1, 2 sc in same sc as last sl st worked. Ch 1, turn.

Rows 2–7: Rep Rows 2–7 of First Petal.

3rd–6th Petal

Rep Second Petal. At end of Row 7 of 6th Petal, finish off and weave in ends.

Trumpet

Note: *Rnds 1 through 6 of Trumpet are worked in continuous rnds. Do not join; mark beg of rnds.*

With Color A, ch 2.

Rnd 1 (RS): 6 sc in 2nd ch from hook.

Rnd 2: 2 sc in each sc—*12 sc*.

Rnd 3: Sc in each sc.

Rnds 4 and 5: Rep Rnd 3.

Rnd 6: Ch 3, sl st in 3rd ch from hook, [sc in next sc, ch 3, sl st in 3rd ch from hook] 11 times; join in next sc. Finish off and weave in ends.

Square

With Color B, ch 4; join to form a ring.

Rnd 1 (RS): Ch 1, 8 sc in ring; join in first sc.

Rnd 2: Ch 3 *(counts as a dc on this and following rnds)*, 2 dc in same sc; ch 2, sk next sc, [3 dc in next sc, ch 2, sk next sc] 3 times; join in 3rd ch of beg ch-3.

Rnd 3: Ch 3, dc in next 2 dc, in next ch-2 sp work (2 dc, ch 2, 2 dc)—*corner made*; *dc in next 3 dc, in next ch-2 sp work (2 dc, ch 2, 2 dc)—*corner made*; rep from * twice more; join in 3rd ch of beg ch-3.

Rnd 4: Ch 4 *(counts as a dc and a ch-1 sp)*, sk next dc, dc in next dc, ch 1, sk next dc, dc in next dc; *in next corner ch-2 sp work corner; dc in next dc, [ch 1, sk next dc, dc in next dc] 3 times; rep from * twice more; in next corner ch-2 sp work corner; dc in next dc, ch 1; join in 3rd ch of beg ch-4. Finish off Color B.

Rnd 5: Join Color C in ch-2 sp of any corner; ch 3, in same sp work (dc, ch 2, 2 dc)—*beg corner made*; *ch 1, sk next dc, dc in next dc, ch 1, [dc in next ch-1 sp, ch 1] 3 times; sk next dc, dc in next dc, ch 1, corner in next corner; rep from * twice more; ch 1, sk next dc, dc in next dc, ch 1, [dc in next ch-1 sp, ch 1] 3 times; sk next dc, dc in next dc, ch 1; join in 3rd ch of beg ch-3.

Rnd 6: Ch 1, sc in same ch and in next dc; 3 sc in next corner ch-2 sp—*sc corner made*; *working in each dc and in each ch-1 sp, sc in next 15 sts, 3 sc in next corner ch-2 sp—*sc corner made*; rep from * twice more; sc in next 13 sts; join in first sc.

Finish off and weave in all ends.

Finishing

With tapestry needle, tack Petal section to Square. Tack Trumpet in center of Petals. ●

Square 6

Materials

- Yarn—Color A off white; Color B turquoise; Color C dark turquoise

Instructions

Square

With Color A, ch 6; join to form a ring.

Rnd 1 (RS): Ch 3 *(counts as a dc on this and following rnds)*, 2 dc in ring; ch 1, [3 dc in ring, ch 1] 7 times; join in 3rd ch of beg ch-3—*8 ch-1 sps*.

Rnd 2: Sl st in next 2 dc and in next ch-1 sp, ch 3, in same sp work (2 dc, ch 3, 3 dc)—*beg corner made*; sc in next ch-1 sp; *in next ch-1 sp work (3 dc, ch 3, 3 dc)—*corner made*; sc in next ch-1 sp; rep from * twice more; join in 3rd ch of beg ch-3.

Rnd 3: Sl st in next 2 dc and in next ch-3 sp, beg corner in same sp; ch 1, 3 dc in next sc; ch 1; *in next corner ch-3 sp work corner; ch 1, 3 dc in next sc; ch 1; rep from * twice more; join in 3rd ch of beg ch-3.

Rnd 4: Ch 3, dc in next 2 dc, 7 dc in next corner ch-3 sp—*dc corner made*; [dc in next 3 dc, dc in next ch-1 sp] twice; *dc in next 3 dc, 7 dc in next corner ch-3 sp—*dc corner made*; [dc in next 3 dc, dc in next ch-1 sp] twice; rep from * twice more; join in 3rd ch of beg ch-3. Finish off Color A.

Rnd 5: Join Color B in 4th dc of any corner; ch 1, 3 sc in same dc—*sc corner made*; sc in next 17 dc; *3 sc in next dc—*sc corner made*; sc in next 17 dc; rep from * twice more; join in first sc. Finish off Color B.

Rnd 6: Join Color C in 2nd sc of any corner; ch 1, sc corner in same sc; sc in next 19 sc; *in next sc work sc corner; sc in next 19 sc; rep from * twice more; join in first sc.

Finish off and weave in all ends.

Butterfly
With Color C, ch 6.

Row 1: Sc in 2nd ch from hook and in each rem ch—*5 sc*. Ch 3 *(counts as first dc on following rows)*, turn.

Row 2 (RS): 2 dc in first sc; [ch 3, sk next sc, 3 dc in next sc] twice. Ch 3, turn.

Row 3: 2 dc in first dc; *ch 3, in next ch-3 sp work (3 dc, ch 3, 3 dc); rep from * once more; ch 3, sk next 2 dc, 3 dc in 3rd ch of turning ch-3. Ch 3, turn.

Row 4: 4 dc in first dc; sc in next ch-3 sp, [9 dc in next ch-3 sp, sc in next ch-3 sp] twice; sk next 2 dc, 5 dc in 3rd ch of turning ch-3.

Finish off and weave in all ends.

Finishing
Cut 18" length of Color B. Wrap yarn tightly around center (between 9-dc groups) of Butterfly, beg and ending at center back. Tie ends to secure. Referring to photo for placement and with tapestry needle, tack wings of Butterfly to Square. ●

Square 7

Materials
- Yarn—Color A off white; Color B emerald green; Color C red

Note: The red and green wreath in this square will puff out for a dimensional effect.

Pattern Stitches
Beginning Popcorn (beg PC): Ch 3, 4 dc in same sp; drop lp from hook, insert hook in 3rd ch of beg ch-3, draw dropped lp through—*beg PC made*.

Popcorn (PC): 5 dc in sp indicated; drop lp from hook, insert hook in first dc made, draw dropped lp through—*PC made*.

Instructions
With Color A, ch 4.

Rnd 1 (RS): 7 dc in 4th ch from hook *(3 skipped chs count as a dc)*; join in 3rd ch of beg 3 skipped chs—*8 dc*.

Rnd 2: Ch 3 (counts as a dc on this and following rnds), dc in same ch; ch 1, [2 dc in next dc, ch 1] 7 times; join in 3rd ch of beg ch-3—8 ch-1 sps. Finish off Color A.

Rnd 3: Join Color B in any ch-1 sp; **beg PC** (see Pattern Stitches) in same sp; ch 2, [**PC** (see Pattern Stitches) in next ch-1 sp, ch 2] 7 times; join in top of beg PC—8 PCs.

Rnd 4: Sl st in next ch-2 sp, in same sp work (beg PC, ch 1, PC); ch 2; *in next ch-2 sp work (PC, ch 1, PC); ch 2; rep from * 6 times more; join in top of beg PC—16 PCs. Finish off Color B.

Rnd 5: Join Color A in any ch-2 sp; ch 3, dc in same sp; ch 2, 2 dc in next ch-1 sp; ch 2; *2 dc in next ch-2 sp; ch 2, 2 dc in next ch-1 sp; ch 2; rep from * 6 times more; join in 3rd ch of beg ch-3.

Rnd 6: Sl st in next dc and in next ch-2 sp, ch 3, in same sp work (2 dc, ch 2, 3 dc)—beg corner made; *ch 1, [2 dc in next ch-2 sp, ch 1] 3 times; in next ch-2 sp work (3 dc, ch 2, 3 dc)—corner made; rep from * twice more; ch 1, [2 dc in next ch-2 sp, ch 1] 3 times; join in 3rd ch of beg ch-3. Finish off Color A.

Berries

Make 8

Join Color C in 2nd dc of any 2-dc group of Rnd 2; ch 4, sl st in same dc; finish off. For rem berries, rep in 2nd dc of each 2-dc group.

Weave in all ends. ●

Square 8

Materials
- Yarn—Color A dark blue; Color B light gold

Pattern Stitch
Front Post Double Crochet (fpdc): Yo, insert hook from front to back to front around post (see page 98) of st indicated, draw up lp, [yo, draw through 2 lps on hook] twice—fpdc made.

Instructions
With Color A, ch 4; join to form a ring.

Rnd 1 (RS): Ch 1, 8 sc in ring; join in first sc.

Rnd 2: Ch 1, 3 sc in same sc—sc corner made; sc in next sc; *3 sc in next sc—sc corner made; sc in next sc; rep from * twice more; join in first sc.

Rnd 3: Ch 1, sc in same sc; *sc corner in next sc; sc in next 3 sc; rep from * twice more; sc corner in next sc; sc in next 2 sc; join in first sc.

Rnd 4: Ch 1, sc in same sc and in next sc; *sc corner in next sc; sc in next 5 sc; rep from * twice more; sc corner in next sc; sc in next 3 sc; join in first sc.

Rnd 5: Sl st in next sc, ch 3 *(counts as a dc on this and following rnds)*, 2 dc in same sc; sk next sc, sc in next sc, sk next sc; *3 dc in next sc; sk next sc, sc in next sc, sk next sc; rep from * 6 times more; join in 3rd ch of beg ch-3.

Rnd 6: Sl st in next dc, ch 1, sc in same dc; sk next dc, in next sc work (dc, ch 1, dc, ch 1, dc)—*dc corner made*; *sk next dc, sc in next dc, sk next dc, 3 dc in next sc; sk next dc**; sc in next dc, sk next dc, in next sc work (dc, ch 1, dc, ch 1, dc)—*dc corner made*; rep from * twice more, then rep from * to ** once; join in first sc. Finish off Color A.

Rnd 7: Join Color B in first ch-1 sp of any corner; ch 1, sc in same sp, in next dc, and in next ch-1 sp; *5 **fpdc** *(see Pattern Stitch)* around 2nd dc of next 3-dc group on 2nd rnd below; sc in 2nd dc of next 3-dc group on working rnd, 5 fpdc around 2nd dc of next 3-dc group on 2nd rnd below**; sc in next ch-1 sp, in next dc, and in next ch-1 sp; rep from * twice more, then rep from * to ** once; join in first sc. Finish off Color B.

Rnd 8: Join Color A in 2nd sc of any 3-sc group of Rnd 7; ch 3, in same sc work (2 dc, ch 2, 3 dc)—*beg 3-dc corner made*; *3 dc in each of next 2 sc on Rnd 6; in 2nd sc of next 3-sc group on Rnd 7 work (3 dc, ch 2, 3 dc)—*3-dc corner made*; rep from * twice more; 3 dc in each of next 2 sc on Rnd 6; join in 3rd ch of beg ch-3.

Rnd 9: Ch 1, sc in same ch and in next 2 dc; *sc corner in next corner ch-2 sp; sc in next 12 dc; rep from * twice more; sc corner in next corner ch-2 sp; sc in next 9 dc; join in first sc.

Finish off and weave in all ends. ●

Square 9

Materials

- Yarn—Color A purple; Color B gold; Color C light purple

Instructions

With Color A, ch 4; join to form a ring.

Rnd 1 (RS): Ch 1, [sc in ring, ch 3] 8 times; join in first sc—*8 ch-3 sps*. Finish off Color A.

Rnd 2: Join Color B in any ch-3 sp; ch 3 *(counts as a dc on this and following rnds)*, in same sp work (dc, ch 2, 2 dc)—*beg corner made*; 2 dc in next ch-3 sp; *in next ch-3 sp work (2 dc, ch 2, 2 dc)—*corner made*; 2 dc in next ch-3 sp; rep from * twice more; join in 3rd ch of beg ch-3. Finish off Color B.

Rnd 3: Join Color C in any corner ch-2 sp; ch 3, in same sp work (2 dc, ch 3, 3 dc)—*beg 3-dc corner made*; [2 dc in sp between next two 2-dc groups] twice; *in next ch-2 sp work (3 dc, ch 3, 3 dc)—*3-dc corner made*; [2 dc in sp between next two 2-dc groups] twice; rep from * twice more; join in 3rd ch of beg ch-3. Finish off Color C.

Rnd 4: Join Color A in any corner ch-3 sp; ch 1, 3 sc in same sp—*sc corner made*; sc in next 10 dc; *3 sc in next corner ch-3 sp—*sc corner made*; sc in next 10 dc; rep from * twice more; join in first sc.

Finish off and weave in all ends. ●

Square 10

Materials
- Yarn—Color A off white; Color B light turquoise; Color C dark turquoise

Instructions
With Color A, ch 6.

Row 1 (RS): Dc in 4th ch from hook *(3 beg skipped chs count as a ch-3 sp on this and following rows)* and in next 2 chs—*3 dc*. Ch 6, turn.

Row 2: Dc in 4th ch from hook and in next 2 chs— *beg shell made*; sk next 3 dc, in next ch-3 sp work (sl st, ch 3, 3 dc)—*shell made*—*2 shells*. Ch 6, turn.

Row 3: Dc in 4th ch from hook and in next 2 chs— *beg shell*; shell in ch-3 sp of each of next 2 shells—*3 shells*; change to Color B by drawing lp through; cut Color A. Ch 6, turn.

Row 4: Dc in 4th ch from hook and in next 2 chs—*beg shell*; shell in ch-3 sp of each shell—*4 shells*. Ch 6, turn.

Row 5: Rep Row 4. At end of row—*5 shells*.

Row 6: Dc in 4th ch from hook and in next 2 chs— *beg shell*; shell in each shell—*6 shells*; change to Color C by drawing lp through; cut Color B. Ch 6, turn.

Row 7: Rep Row 4. At end of row—*7 shells*.

Row 8: Dc in 4th ch from hook and in next 2 chs— *beg shell*; shell in each shell—*8 shells*. Ch 1, turn.

Row 9: Sl st in next 3 dc and in next ch-3 sp, ch 3, 3 dc in same sp—*beg shell made*; shell in each of next 6 shells; sl st in ch-3 sp of next shell—*7 shells*. Ch 1, turn.

Row 10: Sl st in next 3 dc and in next ch-3 sp; change to Color B by drawing lp through; cut Color C; beg shell in same sp; shell in each of next 5 shells; sl st in ch-3 sp of next shell—*6 shells*. Ch 1, turn.

Row 11: Sl st in next 3 dc and in next ch-3 sp, beg shell in same sp; shell in each of next 4 shells; sl st in ch-3 sp of next shell—*5 shells*. Ch 1, turn.

Row 12: Sl st in next 3 dc and in next ch-3 sp, beg shell in same sp; shell in each of next 3 shells; sl st in ch-3 sp of next shell—*4 shells*. Ch 1, turn.

Row 13: Sl st in next 3 dc and in next ch-3 sp; change to Color A by drawing lp through; cut Color B; beg shell in same sp; shell in each of next 2 shells; sl st in ch-3 sp of next shell—*3 shells*. Ch 1, turn.

Row 14: Sl st in next 3 dc and in next ch-3 sp, beg shell in same sp; shell in next shell; sl st in ch-3 sp of next shell—*2 shells*. Ch 1, turn.

Row 15: Sl st in next 3 dc and in next ch-3 sp, beg shell in same sp; sl st in ch-3 sp of last shell.

Finish off and weave in all ends. ●

Square 11

Materials
- Yarn—Color A light purple; Color B purple; Color C off white; Color D dark green

Pattern Stitch
Cluster (CL): Keeping last lp of each tr on hook, 3 tr in sp indicated; yo and draw through all 4 lps on hook—*CL made.*

Instructions
With Color A, ch 6; join to form a ring.

Rnd 1 (RS): Ch 5 *(counts as a dc and a ch-2 sp),* [dc in ring, ch 2] 7 times; join in 3rd ch of beg ch-5—*8 ch-2 sps.*

Rnd 2: Sl st in next ch-2 sp, ch 1, in same sp work (sc, dc, tr, dc, sc)—*petal made;* in each rem ch-2 sp work (sc, dc, tr, dc, sc)—*petal made;* join in back lp of first sc—8 petals. Change to Color B by drawing lp through; cut Color A.

Rnd 3: Ch 3, working behind petals of prev rnd, [sl st in back of first sc of next petal, ch 3] 7 times; join in joining sl st—*8 ch-3 sps.*

Rnd 4: Sl st in next ch-3 sp, ch 1, in same sp work (sc, 2 dc, tr, 2 dc, sc)—*petal made;* in each rem ch-3 sp work (sc, 2 dc, tr, 2 dc, sc)—*petal made;* join in first sc—8 petals. Finish off Color B.

Rnd 5: Join Color C between any 2 petals on Rnd 4; ch 4, working behind petals of prev rnd, [sl st between next 2 petals, ch 4] 7 times; join in joining sl st.

Rnd 6: Sl st in next ch-4 sp, ch 1, in same sp work (sc, 2 dc, 3 tr, 2 dc, sc)—*petal made;* in each rem ch-4 sp work (sc, 2 dc, 3 tr, 2 dc, sc)—*petal made;* join in first sc—8 petals. Change to Color D by drawing lp through; cut Color C.

Rnd 7: Ch 1, sc in same sp; ch 5, in first sc of next petal work (**CL**—*see Pattern Stitch,* ch 6, CL)—*corner made;* *ch 5, sc in first sc of next petal, ch 5, in first sc of next petal work (CL, ch 6, CL)—*corner made;* rep from * twice more; ch 5; join in first sc. Finish off Color D.

Rnd 8: Join Color A in any corner ch-6 sp; ch 3 *(counts as a dc),* in same sp work (2 dc, ch 2, 3 dc)—*beg dc corner made;* 5 dc in next ch-5 sp; dc in next sc, 5 dc in next ch-5 sp; *in next corner ch-6 sp work (3 dc, ch 2, 3 dc)—*dc corner made;* 5 dc in next ch-5 sp; dc in next sc, 5 dc in next ch-5 sp; rep from * twice more; join in 3rd ch of beg ch-3. Change to Color B by drawing lp through; cut Color A.

Rnd 9: Ch 1, sc in same ch and in next 2 dc; *3 sc in next corner ch-2 sp—*sc corner made;* sc in next 17 dc; rep from * twice more; 3 sc in next corner ch-2 sp—*sc corner made;* sc in next 14 dc; join in first sc.

Finish off and weave in all ends. ●

Square 12

Materials

- Yarn—Color A pink; Color B off white; Color C dark green

Pattern Stitches

Beginning Puff Stitch (beg puff st): [Yo and draw up lp in same sc] 3 times; yo and draw through all 7 lps on hook—*puff st made*.

Puff Stitch (puff st): Yo, draw up lp in st indicated, [yo, draw up lp in same st] twice; yo and draw through all 7 lps on hook—*puff st made*.

Instructions

With Color A, ch 2.

Rnd 1 (RS): 8 sc in 2nd ch from hook; do not join.

Rnd 2: Working in front lps only, sl st in each sc; join in first sl st. Finish off Color A.

Rnd 3: Join Color B in any unused lp of Rnd 1; ch 1, in same lp work (sc, ch 2, sc)—*corner made*; working in rem unused lps, sc in next lp; *in next lp work (sc, ch 2, sc)—*corner made*; sc in next lp; rep from * twice more; join in first sc. Finish off Color B.

Rnd 4: Join Color C in any sc between corners; in same sc work **beg puff st** *(see Pattern Stitches)*; ch 4; *sk next corner, **puff st** *(see Pattern Stitches)* in next sc; ch 4; rep from * twice more; join in top of beg puff st. Finish off Color C.

Rnd 5: Working in front of ch-4 sps of Rnd 4, join Color B in any corner ch-2 sp of Rnd 3; ch 1, corner in same sp; *sc in next sc on Rnd 3, in next puff st on Rnd 4, and in next sc on Rnd 3; in next corner ch-2 sp work corner; rep from * twice more; sc in next sc on Rnd 3, in next puff st on Rnd 4, and in next sc on Rnd 3; join in first sc. Finish off Color B.

Rnd 6: Join Color A in any corner ch-2 sp; ch 4 *(counts as an hdc and a ch-2 sp)*, hdc in same sp—*beg hdc corner made*; *sc in next sc, [dc in next sc, sc in next sc] twice; in next corner ch-2 sp work (hdc, ch 2, hdc)—*hdc corner made*; rep from * twice more; sc in next sc, [dc in next sc, sc in next sc] twice; join in 2nd ch of beg ch-4. Finish off Color A.

Rnd 7: Join Color B in any corner ch-2 sp; ch 1, in same sp work (sc, ch 3, sc)—*sc corner made*; *ch 2, sk next hdc, [sc in next sc, ch 2, sk next st] 3 times; in next corner ch-2 sp work (sc, ch 3, sc)—*sc corner made*; rep from * twice more; ch 2, sk next hdc, [sc in next sc, ch 2, sk next st] 3 times; join in first sc.

Finish off and weave in all ends. ●

Square 13

Materials
- Yarn—Color A light turquoise; Color B off white; Color C dark turquoise

Pattern Stitches

Front Post Double Crochet (fpdc): Yo, insert hook from front to back to front around post *(see page 98)* of st indicated, draw up lp, [yo, draw through 2 lps on hook] twice—*fpdc made.*

Back Post Double Crochet (bpdc): Yo, insert hook from back to front to back around post *(see page 98)* of st indicated, draw up lp, [yo, draw through 2 lps on hook] twice—*bpdc made.*

Front Post Half Double Crochet (fphdc): Yo, insert hook from front to back to front around post *(see page 98)* of st indicated, draw up lp, yo and draw through all 3 lps on hook—*fphdc made.*

Instructions
With Color A, ch 6.

Rnd 1 (RS): Dc in 6th ch from hook *(5 skipped chs count as a dc and a ch-2 sp)*, ch 2, [dc in same ch, ch 2] 4 times; join in 3rd ch of beg 5 skipped chs—*6 dc.*

Rnd 2: Sl st in next ch-2 sp, ch 1, 3 sc in same sp; **fpdc** *(see Pattern Stitches)* around next dc, [3 sc in next ch-2 sp, fpdc around next dc] 4 times; 3 dc in next ch-2 sp; fpdc around beg 3 skipped chs of prev rnd; join in first sc. Finish off Color A.

Rnd 3: Join Color B in any fpdc; ch 6 *(counts as a dc and a ch-3 sp)*, dc in same fpdc as joining—*beg corner made;* dc in next 5 sts; *in next st work (dc, ch 3, dc)—*corner made;* dc in next 5 sts; rep from * twice more; join in 3rd ch of beg ch-6. Finish off Color B.

Rnd 4: Join Color A in any corner ch-3 sp; ch 3 *(counts as a dc on this and following rnds)*, in same sp work (dc, ch 2, 2 dc)—*beg 2-dc corner made;* **bpdc** *(see Pattern Stitches)* around each of next 7 dc; *in next corner ch-3 sp work (2 dc, ch 2, 2 dc)—*2-dc corner made;* bpdc around each of next 7 dc; rep from * twice more; join in 3rd ch of beg ch-3. Finish off Color A.

Rnd 5: Join Color C in any corner ch-2 sp; ch 1, in same sp work (sc, ch 2, sc)—*sc corner made;* sc in next 3 dc, sk next 2 dc, in next dc work (2 dc, tr, 2 dc); sk next 2 dc, sc in next 3 dc; *in next corner ch-2 sp work (sc, ch 2, sc)—*sc corner made;* sc in next 3 dc, sk next 2 dc, in next dc work (2 dc, tr, 2 dc); sk next 2 dc, sc in next 3 dc; rep from * twice more; join in first sc. Finish off Color C.

Rnd 6: Join Color B in any corner ch-2 sp; beg 2-dc corner in same sp; ch 1, sk next 2 sc, 3 dc in next sc; ch 2, fpdc around next tr; ch 2, sk next 3 sts, 3 dc in next sc; ch 1; *in next corner ch-2 sp work 2-dc corner; ch 1, sk next 2 sc, 3 dc in next sc; ch 2, fpdc around next tr; ch 2, sk next 3 sts, 3 dc in next sc; ch 1; rep from * twice more; join in 3rd ch of beg ch-3. Finish off Color B.

Rnd 7: Join Color A in any corner ch-2 sp; ch 1, sc corner in same sp; sc in next 2 dc, in next ch-1 sp, and in next 3 dc; 2 sc in next ch-2 sp; **fphdc** *(see Pattern Stitches)* around next fpdc; 2 sc in next ch-2 sp; sc in next 3 dc, in next ch-1 sp, and in next 2 dc; *in next corner ch-2 sp work sc corner; sc in next 2 dc, in next ch-1 sp, and in next 3 dc; 2 sc in next ch-2 sp; fphdc around next fpdc; 2 sc in next ch-2 sp; sc in next 3 dc, in next ch-1 sp, and in next 2 dc; rep from * twice more; join in first sc.

Rnd 8: Ch 1, sc in same sc; *3 sc in next ch-2 sp—*3-sc corner made*; sc in next 19 sts; rep from * twice more; 3 sc in next corner ch-2 sp—*3-sc corner made*; sc in next 18 sts; join in first sc.

Finish off and weave in all ends. ●

Square 14

Materials
- Yarn—Color A yellow; Color B light pink; Color C dark pink; Color D dark red

Instructions
With Color A, ch 5; join to form a ring.

Rnd 1 (RS): Ch 1, 10 sc in ring; join in first sc.

Rnd 2: Ch 1, 2 sc in same sc and in each rem sc; join in first sc—*20 sc.*

Rnd 3: Ch 1, sc in same sc and in next 3 sc; 3 sc in next sc; *sc in next 4 sc, 3 sc in next sc; rep from * twice more; join in front lp of first sc—*28 sc.* Change to Color B by drawing lp through; cut Color A.

Rnd 4: Ch 3 *(counts as a dc on this and following rnds)*, 4 dc in same lp; working in front lps only, sk next sc; *5 dc in next sc; sk next sc; rep from * 12 times more; join in 3rd ch of beg ch-3—*14 5-dc groups.* Finish off Color B.

Rnd 5: Working behind 5-dc groups of prev rnd, join Color B in unused lp of 2nd sc of any 3-sc group on Rnd 3; ch 3, 2 dc in same lp—*beg corner made*; working in rem unused lps and back lps of skipped sc, dc in next 6 lps; *3 dc in next lp—*corner made*; dc in next 6 lps; rep from * twice more; join in 3rd ch of beg ch-3.

Rnd 6: Sl st in front lp of next dc; change to Color C by drawing lp through; cut Color B; ch 3, 4 dc in same lp; sk next dc, working in front lps only, *5 dc in next dc; sk next dc; rep from * 16 times more; join in 3rd ch of beg ch-3—*18 5-dc groups.* Finish off Color C.

Rnd 7: Working behind 5-dc groups of prev rnd, join Color C in unused lp of 2nd dc of any corner on Rnd 5; ch 3, 4 dc in same lp—*beg 5-dc corner made*; working in rem unused lps and back lps of skipped dc on Rnd 5, dc in next 8 lps; *5 dc in next lp—*5-dc corner made*; dc in next 8 lps; rep from * twice more; join in 3rd ch of beg ch-3. Change to Color D by drawing lp through; cut Color C.

Rnd 8: Ch 3, 4 dc in same ch; sk next dc, working in front lps only, *5 dc in next dc; sk next dc; rep from * 24 times more; join in 3rd ch of beg ch-3—*26 5-dc groups.* Finish off Color D.

Rnd 9: Working behind 5-dc groups of prev rnd, join Color D in unused lp of 3rd dc of any corner on Rnd 7; beg 5-dc corner in same lp; working in rem unused lps and back lps of skipped dc, dc in next 12 lps; * in next lp work 5-dc corner; dc in next 12 lps; rep from * twice more; join in 3rd ch of beg ch-3.

Rnd 10: Ch 1, sc in same ch and in next dc; 3 sc in next dc—*sc corner made*; *sc in next 16 dc, 3 sc in next dc—*sc corner made*; rep from * twice more; sc in next 14 dc; join in first sc.

Finish off and weave in all ends. ●

Square 15

Materials
- Yarn—Color A dark purple; Color B purple; Color C light purple

Instructions
With Color A, ch 3; join to form a ring.

Rnd 1 (RS): Ch 3 *(counts as a dc on this and following rnds)*, 2 dc in ring; ch 2, [3 dc in ring, ch 2] 3 times; join in 3rd ch of beg ch-3—*4 ch-2 sps*. Finish off Color A.

Rnd 2: Join Color B in any ch-2 sp; ch 1, in same sp work (sc, ch 3, sc)—*sc corner made*; ch 3; *in next ch-2 sp work (sc, ch 3, sc)—*sc corner made*; ch 3; rep from * twice more; join in first sc. Finish off Color B.

Rnd 3: Join Color C in any corner ch-3 sp; ch 3, in same sp work (2 dc, ch 3, 3 dc)—*beg dc corner made*; ch 1, 3 dc in next ch-3 sp; ch 1; *in next corner ch-3 sp work (3 dc, ch 3, 3 dc)—*dc corner made*; ch 1, 3 dc in next ch-3 sp; ch 1; rep from * twice more; join in 3rd ch of beg ch-3. Finish off Color C.

Rnd 4: Join Color A in any corner ch-3 sp; ch 1, sc corner in same sp; ch 3, [sc in next ch-1 sp, ch 3] twice; *in next corner ch-3 sp work sc corner; ch 3, [sc in next ch-1 sp, ch 3] twice; rep from * twice more; join in first sc. Finish off Color A.

Rnd 5: Join Color B in any corner ch-3 sp; beg dc corner in same sp; ch 1, [3 dc in next ch-3 sp, ch 1] 3 times; *dc corner in next sc corner; ch 1, [3 dc in next ch-3 sp, ch 1] 3 times; rep from * twice more; join in 3rd ch of beg ch-3. Finish off Color B.

Rnd 6: Join Color C in any corner ch-3 sp; beg dc corner in same sp; ch 1, [3 dc in next ch-1 sp, ch 1] 4 times; *dc corner in next sc corner; ch 1, [3 dc in next ch-1 sp, ch 1] 4 times; rep from * twice more; join in 3rd ch of beg ch-3.

Finish off and weave in all ends. ●

Square 16

Materials

- Yarn—Color A yellow; Color B blue; Color C white

Instructions

With Color A, ch 9; join to form a ring.

Rnd 1 (RS): Ch 3 *(counts as a dc on this and following rnds)*, 2 dc in ring; ch 6, sl st over side of last dc made; *3 dc in ring; ch 6, sl st over side of last dc made; rep from * 6 times more; join in 3rd ch of beg ch-3—*8 ch-6 sps*. Change to Color B by drawing lp through; cut Color A.

Rnd 2: Sl st in next dc; *12 dc in next ch-6 sp—*petal made*; sl st in 2nd dc of next 3-dc group; rep from * 6 times more; 12 dc in next ch-6 sp—*petal made*; join in first sl st—*8 petals*. Change to Color C by drawing lp through; cut Color B.

Rnd 3: Ch 1, sc in same sl st; ch 5, working behind petals on prev rnd, sc in next sl st, ch 3; *sc in next sl st, ch 5, sc in next sl st, ch 3; rep from * twice more; join in first sc.

Rnd 4: Sl st in next ch-5 sp, ch 3, in same sp work (2 dc, ch 3, 3 dc)—*beg corner made*; 3 dc in next ch-3 sp; *in next ch-5 sp work (3 dc, ch 3, 3 dc)—*corner made*; 3 dc in next ch-3 sp; rep from * twice more; join in 3rd ch of beg ch-3.

Rnd 5: Ch 3, dc in next 2 dc; *in next corner ch-3 sp work (3 dc, ch 2, 3 dc)—*ch-2 corner made*; dc in next 9 dc; rep from * twice more; in next corner ch-3 sp work (3 dc, ch 2, 3 dc)—*ch-2 corner made*; dc in next 6 dc; join in 3rd ch of beg ch-3. Finish off Color C.

Rnd 6: Join Color B in any corner ch-2 sp; ch 1, 3 sc in same sp—*sc corner made*; sc in next 15 dc; *3 sc in next corner ch-2 sp—*sc corner made*; sc in next 15 dc; rep from * twice more; join in first sc.

Finish off and weave in all ends. ●

Square 17

Materials

- Yarn—Color light pink

Pattern Stitch

Back Post Single Crochet (bpsc): Insert hook from back to front to back around post *(see page 98)* of st indicated, draw up lp, yo and draw through 2 lps on hook—*bpsc made*.

Instructions

Ch 6, join to form a ring.

Rnd 1 (RS): Ch 3 *(counts as a dc on this and following rnds)*, 11 dc in ring; join in 3rd ch of beg ch-3—*12 dc*.

Rnd 2: Ch 2 *(counts as an hdc)*, hdc in same ch; 2 hdc in each rem dc; join in 2nd ch of beg ch-2—*24 hdc*.

Rnd 3: Ch 1, sc in same ch; [ch 5, sk next 2 hdc, sc in next hdc] 7 times; ch 5; join in first sc—*8 ch-5 sps*.

Rnd 4: Sl st in next ch-5 sp, ch 1, in same sp work (sc, hdc, 5 dc, hdc, sc)—*petal made*; in each rem ch-5 sp work (sc, hdc, 5 dc, hdc, sc)—*petal made*; join in back lp of first sc—*8 petals*.

Rnd 5: Ch 5, working behind petals of prev rnd and around posts *(see page 98)* of sc on Rnd 3, bpsc *(see Pattern Stitch)* around next sc; [ch 5, bpsc around next sc] 7 times; do not join—*8 ch-5 sps*.

Rnd 6: Sl st in next ch-5 sp, ch 1, in same sp work (sc, hdc, 7 dc, hdc, sc)—*petal made*; in each rem ch-5 sp work (sc, hdc, 7 dc, hdc, sc)—*petal made*; join in back lp of first sc—*8 petals*.

Rnd 7: Ch 7, working behind petals of prev rnd and around posts of sc on Rnd 5, bpsc around next sc; [ch 7, bpsc around next sc] 7 times; do not join—*8 ch-7 sps*.

Rnd 8: Sl st in next ch-7 sp, ch 1, in same sp work (sc, hdc, 9 dc, hdc, sc)—*petal made*; in each rem ch-7 sp work (sc, hdc, 9 dc, hdc, sc)—*petal made*; join in first sc.

Rnd 9: Ch 7 *(counts as a dc and a ch-4 sp)*, sk next 5 sts, in next dc work (dc, ch 4, dc)—*corner made*; *ch 4, sk next 6 sts, dc in next sc, ch 4, sk next 5 sts, sc in next dc, ch 4**; sk next 6 sts, dc in next sc, ch 4, sk next 5

sts, in next dc work (dc, ch 4, dc)—*corner made*; rep from * twice more, then rep from * to ** once; join in 3rd ch of beg ch-7.

Rnd 10: Sl st in next ch-4 sp, ch 3, 3 dc in same sp; ch 1, in next corner ch-4 sp work (2 dc, ch 3, 2 dc)—*ch-3 corner made*; *ch 1, 4 dc in next ch-4 sp; in next ch-4 sp [ch 1, 3 hdc in next ch-4 sp] twice; ch 1**; 4 dc in next ch-4 sp; ch 1, in next corner ch-4 sp work (2 dc, ch 3, 2 dc)—*ch-3 corner made*; rep from * twice more, then rep from * to ** once; join in 3rd ch of beg ch-3.

Rnd 11: Ch 1, sc in same ch; working in each dc, hdc and ch-1 sp, sc in next 6 sts; *5 sc in next corner ch-3 sp—*sc corner made*; sc in next 23 sts; rep from * twice more; 5 sc in next corner ch-3 sp—*sc corner made*; sc in next 16 sts; join in first sc.

Finish off and weave in ends. ●

Square 18

Materials

• Yarn—Color A dark turquoise; Color B red

Instructions

With Color A, ch 4; join to form a ring.

Rnd 1 (RS): Ch 1, 8 sc in ring; join in first sc.

Rnd 2: *Ch 6, sc in 3rd ch from hook and in next ch, hdc in next 2 chs—*petal made*; sl st in next sc; rep from * 7 times more—*8 petals*. Finish off Color A.

Rnd 3: Join Color B in tip of any petal; ch 5 *(counts as a dc and a ch-2 sp)*, dc in same sp—*beg corner made*; ch 4, sl st in tip of next petal, ch 4; *in tip of next petal work (dc, ch 2, dc)—*corner made*; ch 4, sl st in tip of next petal, ch 4; rep from * twice more; join in 3rd ch of beg ch-5.

Rnd 4: Sl st in next ch-2 sp, ch 3, in same sp work (2 dc, ch 2, 3 dc)—*beg 3-dc corner made*; 4 dc in each of next 2 ch-4 sps; *in next corner ch-2 sp work (3 dc, ch 2, 3 dc)—*3-dc corner made*; 4 dc in each of next 2 ch-4 sps; rep from * twice more; join in 3rd ch of beg ch-3.

Rnd 5: Ch 1, sc in same ch as joining and in next 2 dc; 3 sc in next corner ch-2 sp—*sc corner made*; *sc in next 14 dc, 3 sc in next corner ch-2 sp—*sc corner made*; rep from * twice more; sc in next 11 dc; join in first sc.

Finish off and weave in all ends. ●

Square 19

Materials
• Yarn—Color A pink; Color B off white

Instructions
With Color A, ch 4; join to form a ring.

Rnd 1 (RS): Ch 1, 8 sc in ring; join in back lp of first sc.

Rnd 2: Ch 1, sc in same lp; ch 3, working in back lps only, [sc in next sc, ch 3] 7 times; join in first sc—*8 ch-3 sps*.

Rnd 3: Sl st in next ch-3 sp, ch 1, in same sp work (sc, hdc, dc, hdc, sc)—*petal made*; in each rem ch-3 sp work (sc, hdc, dc, hdc, sc)—petal made; join in back lp of first sc—*8 petals*.

Rnd 4: Working behind petals in prev rnd, sl st in back of next dc, ch 1, sc in same sp; ch 3, [sc in back of dc of next petal, ch 3] 7 times; join in first sc—*8 ch-3 sps*.

Rnd 5: Sl st in next ch-3 sp, ch 1, in same sp work (sc, hdc, dc, tr, dc, hdc, sc)—*petal made*; in each rem ch-3 sp work (sc, hdc, dc, tr, dc, hdc, sc)—*petal made*; join in first sc. Finish off Color A.

Rnd 6: Join Color B in tr of any petal; ch 3 *(counts as a dc)*, in same tr work (2 dc, ch 3, 3 dc)—*beg corner made*; in sp between next 2 sc work (dc, ch 1, dc); ch 1, sc in next tr, ch 1, in sp between next 2 sc work (dc, ch 1, dc); *in next tr work (3 dc, ch 3, 3 dc)—*corner made*; in sp between next 2 sc work (dc, ch 1, dc); ch 1, sc in next tr, ch 1, in sp between next 2 sc work (dc, ch 1, dc); rep from * twice more; join in 3rd ch of beg ch-3.

Rnd 7: Ch 1, sc in same ch and in next 2 dc; 3 sc in next corner ch-3 sp—*sc corner made*; *sc in next 15 sts, 3 sc in next corner ch-3 sp—*sc corner made*; rep from * twice more; dc in next 12 sts; join in first sc.

Finish off and weave in all ends. ●

Square 20

Materials
- Yarn—Color A red; Color B dark turquoise; Color C yellow

Instructions
With Color A, ch 6; join to form a ring.

Rnd 1 (RS): Ch 3 *(counts as a dc on this and following rnds)*, 2 dc in ring; ch 1, [3 dc in ring, ch 1] 7 times; join in 3rd ch of beg ch-3—*8 ch-1 sps*. Finish off Color A.

Rnd 2: Join Color B in any ch-1 sp; ch 3, 5 dc in same sp; 6 dc in each rem ch-1 sp; join in 3rd ch of beg ch-3—*48 dc*. Finish off Color B.

Rnd 3: Join Color C between any 2 6-dc groups; ch 1, in same sp work (sc, dc, sc, dc, sc)—*shell made*; ch 2; *between next 2 6-dc groups work (sc, dc, sc, dc, sc)—*shell made*; ch 2; rep from * 6 times more; join in first sc—*8 shells*. Finish off Color C.

Rnd 4: Join Color B in first dc of any shell; ch 3, 5 dc in same dc; sc in next ch-2 sp, sk next sc; *6 dc in next dc; sc in next ch-2 sp, sk next sc; rep from * 6 times more; join in 3rd ch of beg ch-3—*8 6-dc groups*. Change to Color A by drawing lp through; cut Color B.

Rnd 5: Ch 3, dc in same ch; 2 dc in each of next 5 dc—*beg scallop made*; sk next sc; *2 dc in each of next 6 dc—*scallop made*; sk next sc; rep from * 6 times more; join in 3rd ch of beg ch-3—*8 scallops*. Finish off Color A.

Rnd 6: Join Color B in sp between 3rd and 4th 2-dc groups of any scallop; ch 1, sc in same sp; working in sps between 2-dc groups, [ch 2, sc in next sp] twice; *ch 2, sk next sp, sc in next sp, [ch 2, sc in next sp] 4 times; rep from * 6 times more; ch 2, sk next sp, sc in next sp, ch 2, sc in next sp, ch 2; join in first sc.

Rnd 7: Ch 4, in same sc work (2 tr, ch 3, 3 tr)—*beg corner made*; ch 1, sk next 2 ch-2 sps, 5 dc in next ch-2 sp; ch 1, sk next 2 sc, 3 sc in next sc; ch 1, sk next 2 ch-2 sps, 5 dc in next ch-2 sp; ch 1, sk next 2 sc; *in next sc work (3 tr, ch 3, 3 tr)—*corner made*; ch 1, sk next 2 ch-2 sps, 5 dc in next ch-2 sp; ch 1, sk next 2 sc, 3 sc in next sc; ch 1, sk next 2 ch-2 sps, 5 dc in next ch-2 sp; ch 1, sk next 2 sc; rep from * twice more; join in 4th ch of beg ch-4.

Rnd 8: Ch 1, sc in same ch as joining and in next 2 tr; 3 sc in next corner ch-3 sp—*sc corner made*; *working in each st and in each ch, sc in next 23 sts, 3 sc in next corner ch-3 sp—*sc corner made*; rep from * twice more; sc in next 20 sts; join in first sc.

Finish off and weave in all ends. ●

Square 21

Materials
- Yarn—Color A yellow; Color B gold; Color C light purple

Instructions

Square
With Color A, ch 4; join to form a ring.

Rnd 1 (RS): Ch 3 *(counts as a dc on this and following rnds)*, 2 dc in ring; ch 2, [3 dc in ring, ch 2] 3 times; join in 3rd ch of beg ch-3.

Rnd 2: Sl st in next 2 dc and in next ch-2 sp, ch 3, in same sp work (2 dc, ch 2, 3 dc); in each rem ch-2 sp work (3 dc, ch 2, 3 dc); join in 3rd ch of beg ch-3.

Rnd 3: Sl st in next 2 dc and in next ch-2 sp, ch 3, in same sp work (2 dc, ch 2, 3 dc); 3 dc in sp between next two 3-dc groups; *in next ch-2 sp work (3 dc, ch 2, 3 dc); 3 dc in sp between next 2 3-dc groups; rep from * twice more; join in 3rd ch of beg ch-3.

Rnd 4: Ch 3, dc in next 2 dc, in next ch-2 sp work (2 dc, ch 2, 2 dc)—*corner made*; *dc in next 9 dc, in next ch-2 sp work (2 dc, ch 2, 2 dc)—*corner made*; rep from * twice more; dc in next 6 dc; join in 3rd ch of beg ch-3. Finish off Color A.

Rnd 5: Join Color B in any corner ch-2 sp; ch 3, in same sp work (dc, ch 2, 2 dc)—*beg corner made*; dc in next 13 dc; *in next corner ch-2 sp work corner; dc in next 13 dc; rep from * twice more; join in 3rd ch of beg ch-3.

Rnd 6: Ch 1, sc in same ch and in next dc; 3 sc in next corner ch-2 sp—*sc corner made*; *sc in next 17 dc, 3 sc in next corner ch-2 sp—*sc corner made*; rep from * twice more; sc in next 15 dc; join in first sc.

Rnd 7: Ch 1, sc in same ch and in next 2 sc; sc corner in next sc; *sc in next 19 sc, sc corner in next sc; rep from * twice more; sc in next 16 sc; join in first sc.

Rnd 8: Ch 1, sc in same sc and in next 3 sc; sc corner in next sc; *sc in next 21 sc, sc corner in next sc; rep from * twice more; sc in next 17 sc; join in first sc.

Finish off and weave in all ends.

Flower
With Color C, ch 4; join to form a ring.

Rnd 1: Ch 1, [sc in ring, ch 3] 6 times; join in first sc—*6 ch-3 sps*.

Rnd 2: Sl st in next ch-3 sp, ch 1, in same sp work (sc, hdc, 2 dc, hdc, sc)—*petal made*; in each rem ch-3 sp work (sc, hdc, 2 dc, hdc, sc)—*petal made*; join in back of first sc—*6 petals*.

Rnd 3: Working behind petals of prev rnd, sl st in back of corresponding sc in 2nd rnd below, ch 3, [sl st in back of next sc in 2nd rnd below, ch 3] 5 times; join in beg sl st—*6 ch-3 sps*.

Rnd 4: Sl st in next ch-3 sp, ch 1, in same sp work (sc, hdc, 3 dc, hdc, sc)—*petal made*; in each rem ch-3 sp work (sc, hdc, 3 dc, hdc, sc)—*petal made*; join in first sc—*6 petals*. Finish off, leaving a 12" end for sewing.

Finishing
With tapestry needle, tack Flower to center of Square. Weave in all ends. ●

Square 22

Materials
• Yarn—Color light turquoise

Pattern Stitches
Bobble: Keeping last lp of each dc on hook, 4 dc in st indicated; yo and draw through all 5 lps on hook—*bobble made*. Push bobble to right side.

Mini Bobble (mb): Insert hook in st indicated and draw up lp, ch 4, yo and draw through 2 lps on hook—*mb made*. Push mb to right side.

Instructions
Ch 5.

Rnd 1 (RS): Dc in 5th ch from hook (4 skipped chs count as a dc and a ch-1 sp), ch 1, [dc in same ch, ch 1] 6 times; join in 3rd ch of beg 4 skipped chs—*8 ch-1 sps*.

Rnd 2: Sl st in next ch-1 sp, ch 1, in same sp work (sc, ch 2, sc); **bobble** *(see Pattern Stitches)* in next dc; sc in next ch-1 sp, bobble in next dc; *in next ch-1 sp work (sc, ch 2, sc); bobble in next dc; sc in next ch-1 sp, bobble in next dc; rep from * twice more, ending last rep working last bobble in joining sl st; join in first sc—*8 bobbles*.

Rnd 3: Sl st in next ch-2 sp, ch 6 *(counts as a dc and a ch-3 sp on this and following rnds)*, dc in same sp—*beg dc corner made*; [dc in next sc, dc in top of next bobble] twice; dc in next sc; *in next ch-2 sp work (dc, ch 3, dc)—*dc corner made*; [dc in next sc, dc in top of next bobble] twice; dc in next sc; rep from * twice more, ending last rep working last dc in joining sl st; join in 3rd ch of beg ch-6.

Rnd 4: Sl st in next ch-3 sp, ch 1, 3 sc in same sp—*sc corner made*; [**mb** *(see Pattern Stitches)* in next dc, sc in next dc] 3 times; mb in next sc; *3 sc in next corner ch-3 sp—*sc corner made*; [mb in next dc, sc in next dc] 3 times; mb in next sc; rep from * twice more, ending last rep working last mb in joining sl st; join in first sc—*16 mbs*.

Rnd 5: Sl st in next sc, ch 1, sc corner in same sc; [mb in next sc, sc in next mb] 4 times; mb in next sc; *in next sc work sc corner; [mb in next sc, sc in next mb] 4 times; mb in next sc; rep from * twice more, ending last rep working last mb in joining sl st; join in first sc.

Rnd 6: Sl st in next sc, beg dc corner in same sc; dc in next 11 sts; *in next sc work dc corner; dc in next 11 sts; rep from * twice more, ending last rep working last dc in joining sl st; join in 3rd ch of beg ch-6.

Rnd 7: Sl st in next ch-3 sp, ch 1, in same sp work (sc, ch 3, sc)—*ch-3 corner made*; [bobble in next dc, sc in next 2 dc] 4 times; bobble in next dc; *in next corner ch-3 sp work (sc, ch 3, sc)—*ch-3 corner made*; [bobble in next dc, sc in next 2 dc] 4 times; bobble in next dc; rep from * twice more, ending last rep working last bobble in joining sl st; join in first sc—*20 bobbles*.

Rnd 8: Sl st in next ch-3 sp, beg dc corner in same sc; [ch 1, sk next st, dc in next st] 7 times; ch 1; *in next corner ch-3 sp work dc corner; [ch 1, sk next st, dc in next st] 7 times; ch 1; rep from * twice more; join in 3rd ch of beg ch-6.

Rnd 9: Ch 1, sc in same ch as joining; 5 sc in next corner ch-3 sp—*5-sc corner made*; *working in each dc and in each ch-1 sp, sc in next 17 sts, 5 sc in next corner ch-3 sp—*5-sc corner made*; rep from * twice more; sc in next 16 sts; join in first sc.

Finish off and weave in ends. ●

Square 23

Materials
• Yarn—Color off white

Pattern Stitches
Beginning Cluster (beg CL): Ch 2, keeping last lp of each dc on hook, 2 dc in ring or st indicated; yo and draw through all 3 lps on hook—*beg CL made*.

Cluster (CL): Keeping last lp of each dc on hook, 3 dc in sp indicated; yo and draw through all 4 lps on hook—*CL made*.

Instructions
Ch 8, join to form a ring.

Rnd 1 (RS): Beg CL *(see Pattern Stitches)* in ring; ch 3, [**CL** *(see Pattern Stitches)* in ring, ch 3] 7 times; join in top of beg CL—*8 CLs*.

Rnd 2: Sl st in next ch-3 sp, in same sp work (beg CL, ch 3, CL)—*beg corner made*; ch 2, 3 dc in next ch-3 sp; ch 2; *in next ch-3 sp work (CL, ch 3, CL)—*corner* *made*; ch 2, 3 dc in next ch-3 sp; ch 2; rep from * twice more; join in top of beg CL.

Rnd 3: Sl st in next ch-3 sp, beg corner in same sp; ch 2, 2 dc in next ch-2 sp; dc in next 3 dc, 2 dc in next ch-2 sp; ch 2; *in next corner ch-3 sp work corner; ch 2, 2 dc in next ch-2 sp; dc in next 3 dc, 2 dc in next ch-2 sp; ch 2; rep from * twice more; join in top of beg CL.

Rnd 4: Sl st in next ch-3 sp, beg corner in same sp; ch 2, 2 dc in next ch-2 sp; dc in next 7 dc, 2 dc in next ch-2 sp; ch 2; *corner in next corner; ch 2, 2 dc in next ch-2 sp; dc in next 7 dc, 2 dc in next ch-2 sp; ch 2; rep from * twice more; join in top of beg CL.

Rnd 5: Ch 1, sc in same sp; *3 sc in next corner ch-3 sp—*sc corner made*; sc in next CL, 2 sc in next ch-2 sp; sc in next 11 dc, 2 sc in next ch-2 sp; sc in next CL; rep from * twice more; 3 sc in next corner ch-3 sp—*sc corner made*; sc in next CL, 2 sc in next ch-2 sp; sc in next 11 dc, 2 sc in next ch-2 sp; join in first sc.

Finish off and weave in ends. ●

Square 24

Materials
- Yarn—Color A dark blue; Color B light gold

Instructions
With Color A, ch 5; join to form a ring.

Rnd 1 (RS): Ch 4 *(counts as a tr)*, keeping last lp of each tr on hook, 2 tr in ring; yo and draw through all 3 lps on hook—*beg petal made*; ch 3; *keeping last lp of each tr on hook, 3 tr in ring; yo and draw through all 4 lps on hook—*petal made*; ch 3; rep from * 6 times more; join in top of beg petal—*8 petals*. Finish off Color A.

Rnd 2: Join Color B in any ch-3 sp; ch 3 *(counts as a dc)*, in same sp work (2 dc, ch 2, 3 dc)—*beg corner made*; 3 dc in next ch-3 sp; *in next ch-3 sp work (3 dc, ch 2, 3 dc)—*corner made*; 3 dc in next ch-3 sp; rep from * twice more; join in 3rd ch of beg ch-3.

Rnd 3: Ch 1, sc in same ch as joining and in next 2 dc; 3 sc in next corner ch-2 sp—*sc corner made*; *sc in next 9 dc, 3 sc in next corner ch-2 sp—*sc corner made*; rep from * twice more; sc in next 6 dc; join in first sc.

Finish off and weave in all ends. ●

Square 25

Materials
- Yarn—Color A dark turquoise; Color B dark pink; Color C off white

Instructions
With Color A, ch 4; join to form a ring.

Rnd 1 (RS): Ch 3 *(counts as a dc)*, 11 dc in ring; join in 3rd ch of beg ch-3—*12 dc*. Change to Color B by drawing lp through; cut Color A.

Rnd 2: Ch 5 *(counts as a dc and a ch-2 sp)*, [dc in next dc, ch 2] 11 times; join in 3rd ch of beg ch-5—*12 ch-2 sps*.

Rnd 3: Sl st in next ch-2 sp, ch 1, 3 sc in same sp; 3 sc in each rem ch-2 sp; join in first sc—*36 sc*.

Rnd 4: Ch 1, sc in same sc and in next sc; 2 sc in next sc; [sc in next 2 sc, 2 sc in next sc] 11 times; join in first sc—*48 sc*.

Rnd 5: Ch 1, in same sc work (sc, dc); ch 1, in next sc work (dc, sc)—*shell made*; sk next 2 sc; *in next sc work (sc, dc); ch 1, in next sc work (dc, sc)—*shell made*; sk next 2 sc; rep from * 10 times more; join in first sc—*12 shells*. Finish off Color B.

Rnd 6: Join Color C in ch-1 sp of any shell; ch 1, sc in same sp; ch 5, [sc in ch-1 sp of next shell, ch 5] 11 times; join in first sc—*12 ch-5 sps*.

Rnd 7: Sl st in next ch-5 sp, ch 1, 6 sc in same sp; 6 sc in each rem ch-5 sp; join in first sc—*72 sc*.

Rnd 8: Ch 3, 2 dc in same sc—*beg corner made*; hdc in next 4 sc, sc in next 3 sc, sl st in next 3 sc; sc in next 3 sc, hdc in next 4 sc; *3 dc in next sc—*corner made*; hdc in next 4 sc, sc in next 3 sc, sl st in next 3 sc; sc in next 3 sc, hdc in next 4 sc; rep from * twice more; join in 3rd ch of beg ch-3. Change to Color A by drawing lp through; cut Color C.

Rnd 9: Ch 1, sc in same ch as joining; 3 hdc in next dc—*hdc corner made*; *sc in next 19 sts, 3 hdc in next dc—*hdc corner made*; rep from * twice more; sc in next 18 sts; join in first sc.

Finish off and weave in all ends. ●

Square 26

Materials
- Yarn—Color A light gold; Color B emerald green; Color C off white

Pattern Stitches
Beg Cluster (beg CL): Ch 2, keeping last lp of each dc on hook, 2 dc in st indicated; yo and draw through all 3 lps on hook—*beg CL made.*

Cluster (CL): Keeping last lp of each dc on hook, 3 dc in st indicated; yo and draw through all 4 lps on hook—*CL made.*

Instructions
With Color A, ch 4; join to form a ring.

Rnd 1 (RS): Ch 1, 12 sc in ring; join in first sc. Change to Color B by drawing lp through; cut Color A.

Rnd 2: Ch 1, sc in same sc and in each rem sc; join in first sc—*12 sc.*

Rnd 3: Ch 1, sc in same sc; ch 1, [sc in next sc, ch 1] 11 times; join in first sc. Change to Color C by drawing lp through; cut Color B.

Rnd 4: Beg CL (*see Pattern Stitches*) in same sc; ch 3, [**CL** (*see Pattern Stitches*) in next sc, ch 3] 11 times; join in top of beg CL—*12 CLs.* Finish off Color C.

Rnd 5: Join Color A in any ch-3 sp; ch 3, in same sp work (2 dc, ch 3, 3 dc)—*beg corner made*; 3 dc in each of next 2 ch-3 sps; *in next ch-3 sp work (3 dc, ch 3, 3 dc)—*corner made*; 3 dc in each of next 2 ch-3 sps; rep from * twice more; join in 3rd ch of beg ch-3. Finish off Color A.

Rnd 6: Join Color B in any corner ch-3 sp; beg corner in same sp; [3 dc between next two 3-dc groups] 3 times; * in next corner ch-3 sp work corner; [3 dc between next two 3-dc groups] 3 times; rep from * twice more; join in 3rd ch of beg ch-3.

Rnd 7: Ch 1, sc in same ch as joining and in next 2 dc; 3 sc in next corner ch-3 sp—*sc corner made*; *sc in next 15 dc, 3 sc in next corner ch-3 sp—*sc corner made*; rep from * twice more; sc in next 12 dc; join in first sc.

Finish off and weave in all ends. ●

Square 27

Materials
• Yarn—Color blue

Pattern Stitches

Beginning Popcorn (beg PC): Ch 3, 4 dc in st indicated; drop lp from hook, insert hook in 3rd ch of beg ch-3, draw dropped lp through—*beg PC made.*

Popcorn (PC): 5 dc in st indicated; drop lp from hook, insert hook in first dc made, draw dropped lp through—*PC made.*

Instructions
Ch 10, join to form a ring.

Rnd 1 (RS): Beg PC *(see Pattern Stitches)* in ring; ch 1, **PC** *(see Pattern Stitches)* in ring; ch 4; *PC in ring; ch 1, PC in ring; ch 4; rep from * twice more; join in top of beg PC—*8 PCs.*

Rnd 2: Ch 5 *(counts as a dc and a ch-2 sp on this and following rnds)*, dc in top of next PC, ch 2, in next ch-4 sp work (PC, ch 4, PC)—*corner made;* *[ch 2, dc in top of next PC] twice; ch 2, in next ch-4 sp work (PC, ch 4, PC)—*corner made;* rep from * twice more; ch 2; join in 3rd ch of beg ch-5.

Rnd 3: Ch 5, dc in next dc, ch 2, dc in top of next PC, ch 2, in next corner ch-4 sp work corner; ch 2, dc in top of next PC; *[ch 2, dc in next dc] twice; ch 2, dc in top of next PC, ch 2, in next corner ch-4 sp work corner; ch 2, dc in top of next PC; rep from * twice more; ch 2; join in 3rd ch of beg ch-5.

Rnd 4: Ch 5, [dc in next dc, ch 2] twice; dc in top of next PC, ch 2, corner in next corner; ch 2, dc in top of next PC; *[ch 2, dc in next dc] 4 times; ch 2, dc in top of next PC, ch 2, corner in next corner; ch 2, dc in next PC; rep from * twice more; ch 2, dc in next dc, ch 2; join in 3rd ch of beg ch-5.

Rnd 5: Ch 1, sc in same ch as joining; [2 sc in next ch-2 sp, sc in next dc] 3 times; 2 sc in next ch-2 sp; sc in top of next PC, in next corner ch-4 sp work (2 sc, ch 1, 2 sc)—*sc corner made;* sc in top of next PC; *[2 sc in next ch-2 sp, sc in next dc] 6 times; 2 sc in next ch-2 sp; sc in top of next PC, in next corner ch-4 sp work (2 sc, ch 1, 2 sc)—*sc corner made;* sc in top of next PC; rep from * twice more; [2 sc in next ch-2 sp, sc in next dc] twice; 2 sc in next ch-2 sp; join in first sc.

Finish off and weave in ends. ●

Square 28

Materials
- Yarn—Color A light gold; Color B off white; Color C pink

Pattern Stitches

Beginning Cluster (beg CL): Ch 4, keeping last lp of each tr on hook, 2 tr in sp indicated; yo and draw through all 3 lps on hook—*beg CL made.*

Cluster (CL): Keeping last lp of each tr on hook, 3 tr in sp indicated; yo and draw through all 4 lps on hook—*CL made.*

Instructions
With Color A, ch 2.

Rnd 1 (RS): 8 sc in 2nd ch from hook; join in first sc. Change to Color B by drawing lp through; cut Color A.

Rnd 2: Ch 9—*petal made*; [sl st in next sc, ch 9] 7 times—7 petals made; join in joining sl st—*8 petals.*

Rnd 3: Ch 3, working behind petals of prev rnd, [sl st between next 2 petals, ch 3] 7 times; join in joining sl st—*8 ch-3 sps.*

Rnd 4: *Sl st in next ch-3 sp, in same sp work [ch 9, sl st] 3 times—*3-petal group made*; rep from * 7 times more; join in beg sl st—*8 3-petal groups.*

Rnds 5 and 6: Rep Rnds 3 and 4.

Rnd 7: Ch 4, working behind petal groups of prev rnd, [sl st between next 2 petal groups, ch 4] 7 times; join in joining sl st—*8 ch-4 sps.* Finish off Color B.

Rnd 8: Join Color C in any ch-4 sp; in same sp work (**beg CL**—*see Pattern Stitches*, ch 5, **CL**—*see Pattern Stitches*)—*beg corner made*; ch 2, 3 dc in next ch-4 sp; ch 2; *in next ch-4 sp work (CL, ch 5, CL)—*corner made*; ch 2, 3 dc in next ch-4 sp; ch 2; rep from * twice more; join in top of beg CL.

Rnd 9: Sl st in next ch-5 sp, beg corner in same sp; ch 2, [3 dc in next ch-2 sp, ch 2] twice; *in next corner ch-5 sp work corner; ch 2, [3 dc in next ch-2 sp, ch 2] twice; rep from * twice more; join in top of beg CL.

Rnd 10: Sl st in next ch-5 sp, beg corner in same sp; ch 2, [3 dc in next ch-2 sp, ch 2] 3 times; *corner in next corner; ch 2, [3 dc in next ch-2 sp, ch 2] 3 times; rep from * twice more; join in top of beg CL.

Rnd 11: Sl st in next ch-5 sp, ch 1, 7 sc in same sp—*sc corner made*; 2 sc in next ch-2 sp; [sc in next 3 dc, 2 sc in next ch-2 sp] 3 times; * 7 sc in next corner ch-5 sp—*sc corner made*; 2 sc in next ch-2 sp; [sc in next 3 dc, 2 sc in next ch-2 sp] 3 times; rep from * twice more; join in first sc.

Finish off and weave in all ends. ●

Square 29

Materials
- Yarn—Color light purple

Pattern Stitches
Beg Cluster (beg CL): Ch 2, keeping last lp of each dc on hook, 2 dc in ring or st indicated; yo and draw through all 3 lps on hook—*beg CL made.*

Cluster (CL): Keeping last lp of each dc on hook, 3 dc in ring or st indicated; yo and draw through all 4 lps on hook—*CL made.*

Instructions
Ch 6, join to form a ring.

Rnd 1 (RS): Beg CL *(see Pattern Stitches)* in ring; ch 3, [**CL** *(see Pattern Stitches)* in ring, ch 3] 7 times; join in top of beg CL—*8 ch-3 sps.*

Rnd 2: Sl st in next ch-3 sp, in same sp work (beg CL, ch 4, CL)—*beg corner made;* ch 2, 2 dc in next ch-3 sp; ch 2; *in next ch-3 sp work (CL, ch 4, CL)—*corner made;* ch 2, 2 dc in next ch-3 sp; ch 2; rep from * twice more; join in top of beg CL.

Rnd 3: Sl st in next ch-4 sp, beg corner in same sp; ch 2, dc in next ch-2 sp, in next 2 dc, and in next ch-2 sp; ch 2; *in next corner ch-4 sp work corner; ch 2, dc in next ch-2 sp, in next 2 dc, and in next ch-2 sp; ch 2; rep from * twice more; join in top of beg CL.

Rnd 4: Sl st in next ch-4 sp, beg corner in same sp; ch 2, in next ch-2 sp work (dc, ch 1, dc); dc in next 4 dc, in next ch-2 sp work (dc, ch 1, dc); ch 2; *corner in next corner; ch 2, in next ch-2 sp work (dc, ch 1, dc); dc in next 4 dc, in next ch-2 sp work (dc, ch 1, dc); ch 2; rep from * twice more; join in top of beg CL.

Rnd 5: Sl st in next ch-4 sp, beg corner in same sp; ch 2, [dc in next sp, ch 1] twice; sk next dc, dc in next 4 dc, ch 1, sk next dc, dc in next sp, ch 1, dc in next sp, ch 2; *corner in next corner; ch 2, [dc in next sp, ch 1] twice; sk next dc, dc in next 4 dc, ch 1, sk next dc, dc in next sp, ch 1, dc in next sp, ch 2; rep from * twice more; join in top of beg CL.

Rnd 6: Sl st in next ch-4 sp, beg corner in same sp; ch 3, [dc in next ch sp, ch 1] 3 times; sk next dc, dc in next 2 dc, ch 1, sk next dc, [dc in next ch sp, ch 1] twice; dc in next ch-2 sp, ch 3; *corner in next corner; ch 3, [dc in next ch sp, ch 1] 3 times; sk next dc, dc in next 2 dc, ch 1, sk next dc, [dc in next ch sp, ch 1] twice; dc in next ch-2 sp, ch 3; rep from * twice more; join in top of beg CL.

Rnd 7: Sl st in next ch-4 sp, ch 1, 7 sc in same sp—*sc corner made;* 3 sc in next ch-3 sp; [sc in next dc and in next ch-1 sp] 3 times; sc in next 2 dc, [sc in next ch-1 sp and in next dc] 3 times; 3 sc in next ch-3 sp; *7 sc in next corner ch-4 sp—*sc corner made;* 3 sc in next ch-3 sp; [sc in next dc and in next ch-1 sp] 3 times; sc in next 2 dc, [sc in next ch-1 sp and in next dc] 3 times; 3 sc in next ch-3 sp; rep from * twice more; join in first sc.

Finish off and weave in ends. ●

Square 30

Materials
- Yarn—Color A dark gold; Color B yellow

Pattern Stitches

Cluster (CL): [Yo, draw up lp in ring or sp] twice; yo, draw through 4 lps on hook, yo and draw through 2 lps on hook—*CL made.*

Petal stitch (petal st): Yo, draw up lp in each of 2 sps indicated, yo and draw through all 4 lps on hook—*petal st made.*

Instructions
With Color A, ch 5; join to form a ring.

Rnd 1 (RS): Sl st in ring; *CL *(see Pattern Stitches)* in ring; ch 2; rep from * 7 times more; join in top of first CL—*8 ch-2 sps.*

Rnd 2: Sl st in next ch-2 sp, in same sp work (CL, ch 2) twice; in each rem ch-2 sp work (CL, ch 2) twice; join in top of first CL—*16 CLs.* Finish off Color A.

Rnd 3: Join Color B in any ch-2 sp; in same sp work (CL, ch 2, CL)—*corner made;* ch 1; *[**petal st** *(see Pattern Stitches)* over same sp and next sp; ch 1] 4 times; in same sp work (CL, ch 2, CL)—*corner made;* ch 1; rep from * twice more, [petal st over same sp and next sp; ch 1] 3 times; petal st over same sp and same sp as first corner made; ch 1; join in top of first CL.

Rnd 4: Sl st in next ch-2 sp, in same sp work corner; ch 1, [petal st over same sp and next sp, ch 1] 6 times; * in same sp work corner; ch 1, [petal st over same sp and next sp, ch 1] 6 times; rep from * twice more; join in top of first CL.

Rnd 5: Sl st in next ch-2 sp, in same sp work corner; ch 1, [petal st over same sp and next sp, ch 1] 8 times; *corner in same sp; ch 1, [petal st over same sp and next sp, ch 1] 8 times; rep from * twice more; join in top of first CL.

Rnd 6: Sl st in next ch-2 sp, ch 1, 3 sc in same sp—*sc corner made;* *2 sc in each of next 9 ch-1 sps; 3 sc in next corner ch-2 sp—*sc corner made;* 2 sc in each of next 9 ch-1 sps; rep from * twice more; join in first sc.

Finish off and weave in all ends. ●

Square 31

Materials
- Yarn—Color light blue

Pattern Stitches

Front Post Double Crochet (fpdc): Yo, insert hook from front to back to front around post *(see page 98)* of st indicated, draw up lp, [yo, draw through 2 lps on hook] twice—*fpdc made.*

Back Post Double Crochet (bpdc): Yo, insert hook from back to front to back around post *(see page 98)* of st indicated, draw up lp, [yo, draw through 2 lps on hook] twice—*bpdc made.*

Instructions

Ch 4, join to form a ring.

Rnd 1: Ch 3 *(counts as a dc on this and following rnds)*, 11 dc in ring; join in 3rd ch of beg ch-3—*12 dc.*

Rnd 2: Ch 3, **fpdc** *(see Pattern Stitches)* around beg ch-3 of Rnd 1; ***bpdc** *(see Pattern Stitches)* around next dc; fpdc around same dc; rep from * around; join in 3rd ch of beg ch-3.

Rnd 3 (RS): Ch 6 *(counts as a dc and a ch-3 sp on this and following rnds)*, turn; dc in same ch as joining—*beg corner made*; *[ch 1, sk next st, dc in next st] twice; ch 1, sk next st, in next st work (dc, ch 3, dc)—*corner made*; rep from * twice more; [ch 1, sk next st, dc in next st] twice; ch 1, sk next st; join in 3rd ch of beg ch-6.

Rnd 4: Sl st in next ch-3 sp, ch 6, dc in same sp—*beg corner made*; *[ch 2, dc in next ch-1 sp] 3 times; ch 2, in next corner ch-3 sp work (dc, ch 3, dc); rep from * twice more; [ch 2, dc in next ch-1 sp] 3 times; ch 2; join in 3rd ch of beg ch-6.

Rnd 5: Ch 1, sc in same ch; 3 sc in next ch-3 sp—*sc corner made*; *[sc in next dc, 2 sc in next ch-2 sp] 4 times; sc in next dc, 3 sc in next corner ch-3 sp—*sc corner made*; rep from * twice more; [sc in next dc, 2 sc in next ch-2 sp] 4 times; join in first sc.

Finish off and weave in ends. ●

Square 32

Materials

- Yarn—Color A pale blue; Color B blue; Color C light blue

Pattern Stitch

Double Triple Crochet (dtr): Yo 3 times, draw up lp in st indicated, [yo and draw through 2 lps on hook] 4 times—*dtr made.*

Instructions

With Color A, ch 4; join to form a ring.

Rnd 1 (RS): Ch 3 *(counts as a dc on this and following rnds)*, 7 dc in ring; join in 3rd ch of beg ch-3—*8 dc.*

Rnd 2: Ch 6 *(counts as a dc and a ch-3 sp)*, [dc in next dc, ch 3] 7 times; join in 3rd ch of beg ch-6.

Rnd 3: In each ch-3 sp work (sl st, sc, hdc, 2 dc, hdc, sc, sl st)—*petal made*; join in first sl st—*8 petals.* Finish off Color A.

Rnd 4: Working behind petals on prev rnd and around posts *(see page 98)* of dc on Rnd 2, join Color B around post of any dc on Rnd 2; ch 5; *sl st from back to front to back around post of next dc on Rnd 2, ch 5; rep from * 6 times more; join in joining sl st of Color B.

Rnd 5: Sl st in next ch-5 sp, ch 1, in same sp work (sc, hdc, dc, 5 tr, dc, hdc, sc)—*petal made*; in each rem ch-5 sp work (sc, hdc, dc, 5 tr, dc, hdc, sc)—*petal made*; join in first sc—*8 petals.* Finish off Color B.

Rnd 6: Working behind petals on prev rnd in back of sl sts on Rnd 4, join Color C in any sl st on Rnd 4; ch 6, [sl st in next sl st, ch 6] 7 times; join in joining sl st of Color C.

Rnd 7: Sl st in next ch-6 sp, ch 1, in same sp work (sc, hdc, dc, 6 tr, dc, hdc, sc)—*petal made*; in each rem ch-6 sp work (sc, hdc, dc, 6 tr, dc, hdc, sc)—*petal made*; join in first sc—*8 petals.*

Rnd 8: Ch 6 *(counts as a dtr and a ch-1 sp)*, sk next 3 sts, dc in next 4 tr, sk next 3 sts, **dtr** *(see Pattern Stitch)* in next 2 sc, sk next 3 sts, dc in next 4 tr, ch 1, sk next 3 sts; *dtr in next sc, ch 3—*corner sp made*; dtr in next sc, ch 1, sk next 3 sts, dc in next 4 tr, sk next 3 sts, dtr in next 2 sc, sk next 3 sts, dc in next 4 tr, ch 1, sk next 3 sts; rep from * twice more; dtr in next sc, ch 3—*corner sp made*; join in 5th ch of beg ch-6.

Rnd 9: Ch 2 *(counts as an hdc)*, hdc in next ch-1 sp and in next dc; sc in next 8 sts, hdc in next dc, in next ch-1 sp, and in next dtr; *in next corner ch-3 sp work (2 dc, ch 2, 2 dc)—*dc corner made*; hdc in next dtr, in next ch-1 sp, and in next dc; sc in next 8 sts, hdc in next dc, in next ch-1 sp, and in next dtr; rep from * twice more; in next corner ch-3 sp work (2 dc, ch 2, 2 dc)—*dc corner made*; join in 2nd ch of beg ch-2. Change to Color A by drawing lp through; cut Color C.

Rnd 10: Ch 1, sc in same ch as joining and in next 15 sts; 3 sc in next corner ch-2 sp—*sc corner made*; *sc in next 18 sts, 3 sc in next corner ch-2 sp—*sc corner made*; rep from * twice more; sc in next 2 sts; join in first sc.

Finish off and weave in all ends. ●

Square 33

Materials
- Yarn—Color A emerald green; Color B spring green; Color C off white

Instructions
With Color A, ch 6; join to form a ring.

Rnd 1 (RS): Ch 1, 16 sc in ring; join in first sc.

Rnd 2: Ch 1, sc in same sc; in next sc work (sc, ch 3, dc, ch 3, sl st)—*petal made*; *sc in next sc, in next sc work (sc, ch 3, dc, ch 3, sl st)—*petal made*; rep from * 6 times more; join in first sc—*8 petals*. Finish off Color A.

Rnd 3: Join Color B in back lp of dc of any petal; ch 1, sc in same lp; 3 dc in next sc; *sc in back lp of dc of next petal, 3 dc in next sc; rep from * 6 times more; join in first sc.

Rnd 4: Ch 3 *(counts as a dc on this and following rnds)*, in same sc work (2 dc, ch 1, 3 dc)—*beg corner made*; ch 1, 3 dc in next sc; ch 1; *in next sc work (3 dc, ch 1, 3 dc)—*corner made*; ch 1, 3 dc in next sc; ch 1; rep from * twice more; join in 3rd ch of beg ch-3. Finish off Color B.

Rnd 5: Join Color C in any corner ch-1 sp; beg corner in same sp; [ch 1, 3 dc in next ch-1 sp] twice; ch 1; *in next corner ch-1 sp work corner; ch 1, [3 dc in next ch-1 sp, ch 1] twice; rep from * twice more; join in 3rd ch of beg ch-3.

Finish off and weave in all ends. ●

Square 34

Materials
- Yarn—Color A light turquoise; Color B dark turquoise; Color C black

Pattern Stitches
Beginning Popcorn (beg PC): Ch 3, 3 dc in ring or sp indicated; drop lp from hook, insert hook in 3rd ch of beg ch-3, draw dropped lp through—*beg PC made*.

Popcorn (PC): 4 dc in ring or sp indicated; drop lp from hook, insert hook in first dc made, draw dropped lp through—*PC made*.

Instructions

With Color A, ch 6; join to form a ring.

Rnd 1 (RS): Beg PC *(see Pattern Stitches)* in ring; ch 3, [PC *(see Pattern Stitches)* in ring, ch 3] 3 times; join in top of beg PC—*4 PCs and 4 ch-3 sps.*

Rnd 2: Sl st in next ch-3 sp, in same sp work (beg PC, ch 3, PC)—*beg PC corner made;* ch 3; *in next ch-3 sp work (PC, ch 3, PC)—*PC corner made;* ch 3; rep from * twice more; join in top of beg PC. Finish off Color A.

Rnd 3: Join Color B in any corner ch-3 sp; ch 3 *(counts as a dc on this and following rnds)*, in same sp work (2 dc, ch 3, 3 dc)—*beg dc corner made;* 3 dc in next ch-3 sp; * in next corner ch-3 sp work (3 dc, ch 3, 3 dc)—*dc corner made;* 3 dc in next ch-3 sp; rep from * twice more; join in 3rd ch of beg ch-3.

Rnd 4: Sl st in next 2 dc and in next ch-3 sp, beg dc corner in same sp; [3 dc in sp between next two 3-dc groups] twice; *in next corner ch-3 sp work dc corner; [3 dc in sp between next two 3-dc groups] twice; rep from * twice more; join in 3rd ch of beg ch-3. Finish off Color B.

Rnd 5: Join Color C in any corner ch-3 sp; beg dc corner in same sp; [3 dc in sp between next two 3-dc groups] 3 times; *dc corner in next corner; [3 dc in sp between next two 3-dc groups] 3 times; rep from *twice more; join in 3rd ch of beg ch-3.

Rnd 6: Sl st in next 2 dc and in next ch-3 sp, beg dc corner in same sp; [3 dc in sp between next two 3-dc groups] 4 times; *dc corner in next corner; [3 dc in sp between next two 3-dc groups] 4 times; rep from * twice more; join in 3rd ch of beg ch-3.

Rnd 7: Sl st in next 2 dc and in next ch-3 sp, beg dc corner in same sp; [3 dc in sp between next two 3-dc groups] 5 times; *dc corner in next corner; [3 dc in sp between next two 3-dc groups] 5 times; rep from * twice more; join in 3rd ch of beg ch-3. Finish off Color C.

Rnd 8: Join Color B in any corner ch-3 sp; ch 1, 3 sc in same sp—*sc corner made;* sc in next 21 dc; *3 sc in next corner ch-3 sp—*sc corner made;* sc in next 21 dc; rep from * twice more; join in first sc.

Finish off and weave in all ends. ●

Square 35

Materials

- Yarn—Color A dark brown; Color B gold; Color C off white

Instructions

With Color A, ch 5; join to form a ring.

Rnd 1 (RS): Ch 1, 11 sc in ring; join in first sc.

Rnd 2: Ch 1, 2 sc in same sc and in each rem sc; join in first sc—*22 sc.*

Rnd 3: Ch 1, 2 sc in same sc and in next sc; [2 sc in next sc, sc in next 3 sc] 5 times; join in first sc—*28 sc.*

Rnd 4: Ch 1, sc in same sc and in each rem sc; join in first sc. Change to Color B by drawing lp through; cut Color A.

Rnd 5: *Ch 7, sc in 2nd ch from hook, hdc in next ch, dc in next 2 chs, hdc in next ch, sc in next ch—*long petal made*; in next sc work (sl st, ch 4, tr, ch 4)—*petal made*; sl st in next sc; rep from * 13 times more, ending last rep working last sl st in base of first long petal—*14 long petals and 14 petals*. Finish off Color B.

Rnd 6: Join Color C in tip of any long petal; ch 1, sc in same sp; ch 2, tr in tr of next petal, ch 2; *sc in tip of next long petal, ch 2, tr in tr of next petal, ch 2; rep from * 12 times more; join in first sc.

Rnd 7: Sl st in next ch-2 sp, ch 4 *(counts as a tr on this and following rnds)*, in same sp work (2 tr, ch 3, 3 tr)—*beg corner made*; 2 dc in each of next 2 ch-2 sps; 2 hdc in each of next 2 ch-2 sps; 2 dc in each of next 2 ch-2 sps; *in next ch-2 sp work (3 tr, ch 3, 3 tr)—*corner made*; 2 dc in each of next 2 ch-2 sps; 2 hdc in each of next 2 ch-2 sps; 2 dc in each of next 2 ch-2 sps; rep from * twice more; join in 4th ch of beg ch-4.

Rnd 8: Ch 3 *(counts as a dc)*, dc in next 2 tr; *in next corner ch-3 sp work (3 dc, ch 2, 3 dc)—*dc corner made*; dc in next 18 sts; rep from * twice more; in next corner ch-3 sp work (3 dc, ch 2, 3 dc)—*dc corner made*; dc in next 15 sts; join in 3rd ch of beg ch-3.

Rnd 9: Ch 1, sc in same ch as joining and in next 5 dc; *5 sc in next corner ch-2 sp—*sc corner made*; sc in next 24 dc; rep from * twice more; 5 sc in next corner ch-2 sp—*sc corner made*; sc in next 18 dc; join in first sc.

Finish off and weave in all ends. ●

Square 36

Materials
- Yarn—Color A dark pink; Color B light pink; Color C purple

Instructions

Square
With Color A, ch 4; join to form a ring.

Rnd 1 (RS): Ch 3 *(counts as a dc on this and following rnds)*, 2 dc in ring; ch 2, [3 dc in ring, ch 2] 3 times; join in 3rd ch of beg ch-3—*12 dc*.

Rnd 2: Ch 1, sc in same ch as joining; ch 3, sk next dc, sc in next dc, in next ch-2 sp work (sc, ch 3, sc)—*corner made*; *sc in next dc, ch 3, sk next dc, sc in next dc, in next ch-2 sp work (sc, ch 3, sc)—*corner made*; rep from * twice more; join in first sc. Finish off Color A.

Rnd 3: Join Color B in any corner ch-3 sp; ch 3, in same sp work (2 dc, ch 2, 3 dc)—*beg dc corner made*; 3 dc in next ch-3 sp; *in next corner ch-3 sp work (3 dc, ch 2, 3 dc)—*dc corner made*; 3 dc in next ch-3 sp; rep from * twice more; join in 3rd ch of beg ch-3.

Rnd 4: Sl st in next 2 dc and in next ch-2 sp; beg dc corner in same sp; [3 dc between next two 3-dc groups] twice; *in next corner ch-2 sp work dc corner; [3 dc between next two 3-dc groups] twice; rep from * twice more; join in 3rd ch of beg ch-3. Finish off Color B.

Rnd 5: Join Color C in any corner ch-2 sp; ch 1, in same sp work (sc, ch 2, sc)—*sc corner made*; sc in next 12 dc; *in next corner ch-2 sp work (sc, ch 2, sc)—*sc corner made*; sc in next 12 dc; rep from * twice more; join in first sc. Finish off Color C.

Rnd 6: Join Color A in any corner ch-2 sp; ch 1, sc corner in same sp; sc in each sc to next corner ch-2 sp; *sc corner in corner ch-2 sp; sc in each sc to next corner ch-2 sp; rep from * twice more; join in first sc. Finish off Color A.

Rnd 7: With Color C, rep Rnd 6. Finish off Color C.

Flower

Hold Square with right side facing you; join Color B in unused lp of 2nd dc of any 3-dc group on Rnd 1.

Rnd 1: Ch 3, in same dc work (dc, ch 3, sl st)—*beg petal made*; * ch 2, working in unused lps and sps of Rnd 1 of Square, in next corner ch-2 sp work (sl st, ch 3, dc, ch 3, sl st)—*petal made*; ch 2, in unused lp of 2nd dc of next 3-dc group work (sl st, ch 3, dc, ch 3, sl st)—*petal made*; rep from * twice more; ch 2, in next corner ch-2 sp of Rnd 1 of Square work (sl st, ch 3, dc, ch 3, sl st)—*petal made*; ch 2; join in joining sl st—*8 petals*. Finish off Color B.

Rnd 2: Join Color A in any ch-2 sp of Rnd 1 of Flower; beg petal in same sp; ch 2, working behind petals of prev rnd, [petal in next ch-2 sp, ch 2] 7 times; join in joining sl st. Finish off Color A.

Rnd 3: Join Color C in any ch-2 sp of Rnd 2 of Flower; ch 1, in same sp work (sc, ch 8, sc); ch 2; *working behind petals of prev rnd, in next ch-2 sp work (sc, ch 8, sc); ch 2; rep from * 6 times more; join in first sc.

Finish off and weave in all ends. ●

Square 37

Materials
- Yarn—Color A off white; Color B green; Color C pink

Pattern Stitch
Long Single Crochet (long sc): Insert hook in st indicated in 2nd rnd below, draw up lp to height of working rnd, yo and draw through 2 lps on hook—*long sc made*.

Instructions

Square
With Color A, ch 4; join to form a ring.

Rnd 1 (RS): Sl st in ring, ch 3 *(counts as a dc on this and following rnds)*, 2 dc in ring; ch 2, [3 dc in ring, ch 2] 3 times; join in 3rd ch of beg ch-3.

Rnd 2: Sl st in next 2 dc and in next ch-2 sp, ch 3, in same sp work (2 dc, ch 2, 3 dc)—*beg corner made*; *in next ch-2 sp work (3 dc, ch 2, 3 dc)—*corner made*; rep from * twice more; join in 3rd ch of beg ch-3.

Rnd 3: Sl st in next 2 dc and in next ch-2 sp, beg corner in same sp; 3 dc in sp between next two 3-dc groups; *in next corner ch-2 sp work corner; 3 dc in sp between next two 3-dc groups; rep from * twice more; join in 3rd ch of beg ch-3. Finish off Color A.

Rnd 4: Join Color B in any corner ch-2 sp; ch 3, in same sp work (dc, ch 2, 2 dc)—*beg 2-dc corner made*; [dc in next 3 dc and in sp between last dc worked and next dc] twice; dc in next 3 dc; * in next corner ch-2 sp work (2 dc, ch 2, 2 dc)—*2-dc corner made*; [dc in next 3 dc and in sp between last dc worked and next dc] twice; dc in next 3 dc; rep from * twice more; join in 3rd ch of beg ch-3.

Rnd 5: Ch 3, dc in next dc, 2-dc corner in next corner; *dc in next 15 dc, 2-dc corner in next corner; rep from * twice more; dc in next 13 dc; join in 3rd ch of beg ch-3.

Rnd 6: Ch 1, sc in same ch and in next 3 dc; 3 sc in next corner ch-2 sp—**sc corner made**; *sc in next 19 dc, 3 sc in next corner ch-2 sp—*sc corner made*; rep from * twice more; sc in next 15 sc; join in first sc.

Rnd 7: Ch 1, sc in same sc and in next 4 sc; sc corner in next sc; *sc in next 21 sc, sc corner in next sc; rep from * twice more; sc in next 16 sc; join in first sc.

Rnd 8: Ch 1, sc in same sc and in next 5 sc; sc corner in next sc; *sc in next 23 sc, sc corner in next sc; rep from * twice more; sc in next 17 sc; join in first sc. Finish off Color B.

Rnd 9: Join Color C in 2nd sc after any sc corner; ch 1, sc in same sc; [**long sc** *(see Pattern Stitch)* in next sc in 2nd rnd below, on working rnd, sk corresponding sc, sc in next sc] 10 times; *in 2nd sc of next sc corner on 2nd rnd below work (2 long sc, ch 2, 2 long sc)—*long sc corner made*; on working rnd, sk next 4 sc, sc in next sc; [long sc in next sc in 2nd rnd below, on working rnd, sk corresponding sc, sc in next sc] 10 times; rep from * twice more; in 2nd sc of next sc corner on 2nd rnd below work (2 long sc, ch 2, 2 long sc)—*long sc corner made*; join in first sc

Rnd 10: Ch 1, sc in same sc; working in each long sc and in each sc, sc in next 22 sts; *sc corner in next corner; sc in next 25 sts; rep from * twice more; sc corner in next corner; sc in next 2 sts; join in first sc.

Finish off and weave in all ends.

Flower

With Color C, ch 4; join to form a ring.

Rnd 1: Ch 1, [sc in ring, ch 4] 6 times; join in first sc.

Rnd 2: Ch 1, sc in same sc; *in next ch-4 sp work (sc, hdc, 2 dc, hdc, sc)—*petal made*; sc in next sc; rep from * 5 times more, ending last rep without working last sc; join in back of first sc—*6 petals*.

Rnd 3: Ch 4, working behind petals of prev rnd, [sl st in back of sc between next 2 petals, ch 4] 5 times; join in joining sl st—*6 ch-4 sps*.

Rnd 4: Sl st in next ch-4 sp, ch 1, in same sp work (sc, hdc, 3 dc, hdc, sc)—*petal made*; in each rem ch-4 sp work (sc, hdc, 3 dc, hdc, sc)—*petal made*; join in first sc—*6 petals*.

Finish off and weave in all ends.

Finishing

With tapestry needle, tack Flower to center of Square. ●

Square 38

dc, hdc)—*petal made*; rep from * 6 times; join in first sc—*8 petals*. Finish off Color B.

Rnd 4: Join Color A in dtr of any petal; ch 6 *(counts as a dc and a ch-3 sp)*, dc in same dtr—*beg corner made*; ch 5, sc in dtr of next petal, ch 5; *in dtr of next petal work (dc, ch 3, dc)—*corner made*; ch 5, sc in dtr of next petal, ch 5; rep from * twice more; join in 3rd ch of beg ch-6.

Rnd 5: Ch 1, sc in same ch; in next corner ch-3 sp work (3 sc, ch 1, 3 sc)—*sc corner made*; *sc in next dc, 6 sc in next ch-5 sp; sc in next sc, 6 sc in next ch-5 sp; sc in next dc, in next corner ch-3 sp work (3 sc, ch 1, 3 sc)—*sc corner made*; rep from * twice more; sc in next dc, 6 sc in next ch-5 sp, sc in next sc, 6 sc in next ch-5 sp; join in first sc.

Finish off and weave in all ends. ●

Materials
- Yarn—Color A yellow; Color B light purple

Pattern Stitch
Double Triple Crochet (dtr): Yo 3 times, draw up lp in st indicated, [yo, draw through 2 lps on hook] 4 times—*dtr made*.

Instructions
With Color A, ch 12; join to form a ring.

Rnd 1 (RS): Ch 3 *(counts as a dc)*, 23 dc in ring; join in 3rd ch of beg ch-3—*24 dc*. Finish off Color A.

Rnd 2: Join Color B in sp between any 2 dc; ch 1, sc in same sp; ch 3; *sk next 3 dc, sc in sp between last skipped dc and next dc, ch 3; rep from * 6 times more; join in first sc—*8 ch-3 sps*.

Rnd 3: Ch 1, sc in same sc; in next ch-3 sp work (hdc, dc, tr, **dtr**—*see Pattern Stitch*, tr, dc, hdc)—*petal made*; *sc in next sc, in next ch-3 sp work (hdc, dc, tr, dtr, tr,

Square 39

Materials
- Yarn—Color A yellow; Color B light turquoise; Color C dark turquoise

Pattern Stitches

Beginning Puff Stitch (beg puff st): Draw up lp in sp indicated, [yo, draw up lp in same sp] 4 times; yo and draw through all 10 lps on hook—*beg puff st made.*

Puff Stitch (puff st): Yo, draw up lp in sp indicated, [yo, draw up lp in same sp] 3 times; yo and draw through all 9 lps on hook—*puff st made.*

Instructions

With Color A, ch 5; join to form a ring.

Rnd 1 (RS): Ch 3 *(counts as a dc on this and following rnds)*, 15 dc in ring; join in 3rd ch of beg ch-3—*16 dc.* Finish off Color A.

Rnd 2: Join Color B in sp between any 2 dc; ch 5 *(counts as a dc and a ch-2 sp)*, [dc in sp between next 2 dc, ch 2] 15 times; join in 3rd ch of beg ch-5.

Rnd 3: Sl st in next ch-2 sp, **beg puff st** *(see Pattern Stitches)* in same sp; ch 2; ***puff st** *(see Pattern Stitches)* in next ch-2 sp; ch 2; rep from * 14 times more; join in top of first puff st—*16 puff sts.* Finish off Color B.

Rnd 4: Join Color C in any ch-2 sp; ch 4 *(counts as a tr)*, in same sp work (2 tr, ch 1, 3 tr)—*beg corner made*; [ch 1, 2 dc in next ch-2 sp] 3 times; ch 1; *in next ch-2 sp work (3 tr, ch 1, 3 tr)—*corner made*; [ch 1, 2 dc in next ch-2 sp] 3 times; ch 1; rep from * twice more; join in 4th ch of beg ch-4.

Rnd 5: Ch 1, sc in same ch and in next 2 tr; 3 sc in next corner ch-1 sp—*sc corner made*; *sc in next 3 tr and in next ch-1 sp, [sc in next 2 dc and in next ch-1 sp] 3 times; sc in next 3 tr, 3 sc in next corner ch-1 sp—*sc corner made*; rep from * twice more; sc in next 3 tr and in next ch-1 sp, [sc in next 2 dc and in next ch-1 sp] 3 times; join in first sc.

Finish off and weave in all ends. ●

Square 40

Materials

• Yarn—Color A off white; Color B light blue; Color C red

Instructions

With Color A, ch 8; join to form a ring.

Rnd 1 (RS): Ch 3 *(counts as a dc on this and following rnds)*, 15 dc in ring; join in 3rd ch of beg ch-3—*16 dc.*

Rnd 2: Ch 5 *(counts as a dc and a ch-2 sp)*, [dc in next dc, ch 2] 15 times; join in 3rd ch of beg ch-5—*16 ch-2 sps.* Finish off Color A.

Rnd 3: Join Color B in any ch-2 sp; ch 3, 2 dc in same sp; ch 1, [3 dc in next ch-2 sp, ch 1] 15 times; join in 3rd ch of beg ch-3—*16 3-dc groups.*

Rnd 4: Sl st in next 2 dc and in next ch-1 sp, ch 1, sc in same sp; ch 6—*corner lp made*; *[sc in next ch-1 sp, ch 3] 3 times; sc in next ch-1 sp, ch 6—*corner lp made*; rep from * twice more; [sc in next ch-1 sp, ch 3] 3 times; join in first sc. Finish off Color B.

Rnd 5: Join Color C in any corner lp; ch 3, in same lp work (4 dc, ch 2, 5 dc)—*beg corner made*; 3 dc in each of next 3 ch-3 sps; *in next corner lp work (5 dc, ch 2, 5 dc)—*corner made*; 3 dc in each of next 3 ch-3 sps; rep from * twice more; join in 3rd ch of beg ch-3. Finish off Color C.

Rnd 6: Join Color B in any corner ch-2 sp; ch 3, in same sp work (dc, ch 1, 2 dc)—*beg 2-dc corner made*; dc in next 19 dc; *in next corner ch-2 sp work (2 dc, ch 1, 2 dc)—*2-dc corner made*; dc in next 19 dc; rep from * twice more; join in 3rd ch of beg ch-3.

Finish off and weave in all ends. ●

Square 41

Materials
- Yarn—Color red

Pattern Stitch
Puff Stitch (puff st): Yo, draw up lp in sp indicated, yo, draw up lp in same sp, yo and draw through all 5 lps on hook—*puff st made*.

Instructions
Ch 6, join to form a ring.

Rnd 1 (RS): Ch 3 *(counts as a dc on this and following rnds)*, 2 dc in ring; ch 3, [3 dc in ring, ch 3] 3 times; join in 3rd ch of beg ch-3—*12 dc*.

Rnd 2: Ch 3, dc in next 2 dc, ch 1, in next ch-3 sp work (**puff st** —*see Pattern Stitch*, ch 4, puff st)—*corner made*; ch 1; *dc in next 3 dc, ch 1, in next ch-3 sp work (puff st, ch 4, puff st)—*corner made*; ch 1; rep from * twice more; join in 3rd ch of beg ch-3.

Rnd 3: Ch 3, dc in next 2 dc and in next puff st, ch 1, in next corner ch-4 sp work (puff st, ch 5, puff st)—*ch-5 corner made*; ch 1; *dc in next puff st, in next 3 dc and in next puff st; ch 1, in next corner ch-4 sp work (puff st, ch 5, puff st)—*ch-5 corner made*; ch 1; rep from * twice more; dc in next puff st; join in 3rd ch of beg ch-3.

Rnd 4: Ch 3, dc in next 3 dc and in next puff st, ch 1, in next corner ch-5 sp work ch-5 corner; ch 1; *dc in next puff st, in next 5 dc, and in next puff st; ch 1, in next corner ch-5 sp work ch-5 corner; ch 1; rep from * twice more; dc in next puff st and in next dc; join in 3rd ch of beg ch-3.

Rnd 5: Ch 3, dc in next 4 dc and in next puff st, ch 1, ch-5 corner in next corner; ch 1; *dc in next puff st, in next 7 dc, and in next puff st; ch 1, ch-5 corner in next corner; ch 1; rep from * twice more; dc in next puff st and in next 2 dc; join in 3rd ch of beg ch-3.

Rnd 6: Ch 1, sc in same ch, in next 5 dc, in next ch-1 sp, and in next puff st; *5 sc in next corner ch-5 sp—*sc corner made*; sc in next puff st, in next ch-1 sp, in next 9 dc, in next ch-1 sp, and in next puff st; rep from * twice more; 5 sc in next corner ch-5 sp—*sc corner made*; sc in next puff st, in next ch-1 sp, and in next 3 dc; join in first sc.

Finish off and weave in ends. ●

Square 42

Materials

- Yarn—Color turquoise

Pattern Stitches

Beginning Puff Stitch (beg puff st): Draw up lp in sp or st indicated, [yo, draw up lp in same sp or st] 3 times; yo and draw through all 8 lps on hook—*beg puff st made.*

Puff Stitch (puff st): Yo, draw up lp in sp or st indicated, [yo, draw up lp in same sp or st] twice; yo and draw through all 7 lps on hook—*puff st made.*

Instructions

Ch 6, join to form a ring.

Rnd 1 (RS): **Beg puff st** (see Pattern Stitches) in ring; ch 1, [**puff st** (see Pattern Stitches) in ring, ch 1] 7 times; join in top of beg puff st—*8 puff sts.*

Rnd 2: Sl st in next ch-1 sp, in same sp work (beg puff st, ch 1, puff st); ch 3; *in next ch-1 sp work (puff st, ch 1, puff st); ch 3; rep from * 6 times more; join in top of beg puff st—*16 puff sts.*

Rnd 3: Sl st in next ch-1 sp, beg puff st in same sp; ch 3, sk next ch-3 sp, [puff st in next ch-1 sp, ch 3, sk next ch-3 sp] 7 times; join in top of beg puff st—*8 puff sts.*

Rnd 4: Beg puff st in same puff st, ch 1, in next ch-3 sp work (puff st, ch 3, puff st)—*corner made;* *ch 1, puff st in next puff st; ch 1, puff st in next ch-3 sp; ch 1, puff st in next puff st; ch 1, in next ch-3 sp work (puff st, ch 3, puff st)—*corner made;* rep from * twice more; ch 1, puff st in next puff st; ch 1, puff st in next ch-3 sp; ch 1; join in top of beg puff st.

Rnd 5: Sl st in next ch-1 sp, beg puff st in same sp; ch 1, in next corner ch-3 sp work corner; *ch 1, [puff st in next ch-1 sp, ch 1] 4 times; in next corner ch-3 sp work corner; rep from * twice more; ch 1, [puff st in next ch-1 sp, ch 1] 3 times; join in top of beg puff st.

Rnd 6: Sl st in next ch-1 sp, beg puff st in same sp; ch 1, corner in next corner; *ch 1, [puff st in next ch-1 sp, ch 1] 5 times; corner in next corner; rep from * twice more; ch 1, [puff st in next ch-1 sp, ch 1] 4 times; join in top of beg puff st.

Rnd 7: Ch 1, sc in same puff st, in next ch-1 sp, and in next puff st; *5 sc in next corner ch-3 sp—*sc corner made;* [sc in next puff st and in next ch-1 sp] 6 times; sc in next puff st; rep from * twice more; 5 sc in next corner ch-3 sp—*sc corner made;* [sc in next puff st and in next ch-1 sp] 5 times; join in first sc.

Finish off and weave in ends. ●

Square 43

Materials
• Yarn—Color light purple

Pattern Stitches
Beginning Popcorn (beg PC): Ch 3, 4 dc in st indicated; drop lp from hook, insert hook in 3rd ch of beg ch-3, draw dropped lp through—*beg PC made.*

Popcorn (PC): 5 dc in ring or st indicated; drop lp from hook, insert hook in first dc made, draw dropped lp through—*PC made.*

Instructions
Ch 6, join to form a ring.

Rnd 1 (RS): Ch 3 *(counts as a dc on this and following rnds)*, in ring work (dc, **PC**—*see Pattern Stitches*, 2 dc); ch 2; *in ring work (2 dc, PC, 2 dc); ch 2; rep from * twice more; join in 3rd ch of beg ch-3—*4 PCs and 16 dc.*

Rnd 2: Ch 3, working in each dc and in top of each PC, dc in next 4 sts, in next ch-2 sp work (dc, ch 3, dc)—*corner made*; *dc in next 5 sts, in next ch-2 sp work (dc, ch 3, dc)—*corner made*; rep from * twice more; join in 3rd ch of beg ch-3.

Rnd 3: Ch 3, PC in next dc; dc in next dc, PC in next dc; dc in next 2 dc; *in next corner ch-3 sp work corner; dc in next 2 dc, PC in next dc; dc in next dc, PC in next dc; dc in next 2 dc; rep from * twice more; in next corner ch-3 sp work corner; dc in next dc; join in 3rd ch of beg ch-3.

Rnd 4: Ch 3, working in each dc and in top of each PC, dc in next 6 sts, in next corner ch-3 sp work (dc, ch 4, dc)—*ch-4 corner made*; *dc in next 9 sts, in next corner ch-3 sp work (dc, ch 4, dc)—*ch-4 corner made*; rep from * twice more; dc in next 2 dc; join in 3rd ch of beg ch-3.

Rnd 5: Beg PC *(see Pattern Stitches)* in same ch; [dc in next dc, PC in next dc] twice; dc in next 3 dc; *ch-4 corner in next corner; dc in next 3 dc, PC in next dc; [dc in next dc, PC in next dc] twice; dc in next 3 dc; rep from * twice more; ch-4 corner in next corner; dc in next 3 dc; join in top of beg PC.

Rnd 6: Ch 3, dc in next 8 sts, in next corner ch-4 sp work (dc, ch 5, dc)—*ch-5 corner made*; *dc in next 13 sts, in next corner ch-4 sp work (dc, ch 5, dc)—*ch-5 corner made*; rep from * twice more; dc in next 4 dc; join in 3rd ch of beg ch-3.

Rnd 7: Ch 3, dc in next 9 dc, in next corner ch-5 sp work (3 dc, tr, 3 dc)—*tr corner made*; * dc in next 15 dc, in next corner ch-5 sp work (3 dc, tr, 3 dc)—*tr corner made*; rep from * twice more; dc in next 5 dc; join in 3rd ch of beg ch-3.

Rnd 8: Ch 1, sc in same ch and in next 12 dc; 3 sc in next tr—*sc corner made*; *sc in next 21 dc, 3 sc in next tr—*sc corner made*; rep from * twice more; sc in next 8 dc; join in first sc.

Finish off and weave in ends. ●

Square 44

Materials

- Yarn—Color A off white; Color B blue; Color C pink

Instructions

With Color A, ch 12.

Row 1 (WS): Dc in 6th ch from hook *(5 skipped chs count as a ch-1 sp, a dc, and a ch-1 sp)*; [ch 1, sk next ch, dc in next ch] 3 times. Ch 4 *(counts as first dc and ch-1 sp on following rows)*, turn.

Row 2 (RS): Dc in next dc, [ch 1, dc in next dc] twice; ch 1, sk next ch, dc in next ch. Ch 4, turn.

Rows 3 and 4: Rep Row 2. At end of Row 4, do not ch 4. Finish off Color A.

Hold piece with RS facing you and Row 4 at top; join Color B in upper right-hand corner sp.

Rnd 1: Ch 3 *(counts as a dc)*, in same sp work (2 dc, ch 1, 3 dc)—*beg corner made*; working across Row 4, 3 dc in each of next 2 ch-1 sps; in next sp work (3 dc, ch 1, 3 dc)—*corner made*; working along side in sps formed by edge dc and turning chs, 3 dc in each of next 2 sps; in next sp work (3 dc, ch 1, 3 dc)—*corner made*; working across beg ch, 3 dc in each of next 2 ch-1 sps; in next sp work (3 dc, ch 1, 3 dc)—*corner made*; working along side in sps formed by edge dc and turning chs, 3 dc in each of next 2 sps; join in 3rd ch of beg ch-3. Finish off Color B.

Rnd 2: Join Color C in any corner ch-1 sp; ch 4 *(counts as a dc and a ch-1 sp)*, dc in same sp—*beg dc corner made*; dc in next 12 dc; *in next corner ch-1 sp work (dc, ch 1, dc)—*dc corner made*; dc in next 12 dc; rep from *twice more; join in 3rd ch of beg ch-4.

Finish off and weave in all ends. ●

Square 45

Materials

- Yarn—Color A light yellow; Color B gold; Color C dark green

Pattern Stitches

Beginning Puff Stitch (beg puff st): Draw up lp in sp indicated, [yo, draw up lp in same sp] 3 times; yo and draw through all 8 lps on hook—*beg puff st made.*

Puff Stitch (puff st): Yo, draw up lp in sp indicated, [yo, draw up lp in same sp] twice; yo and draw through all 7 lps on hook—*puff st made.*

Instructions

With Color A, ch 5; join to form a ring.

Rnd 1 (RS): Ch 5 *(counts as a tr and a ch-1 sp)*, [tr in ring, ch 1] 11 times; join in 4th ch of beg ch-5—*12 ch-1 sps*. Finish off Color A.

Rnd 2: Join Color B in any ch-1 sp; in same sp work (**beg puff st** —*see Pattern Stitches*, ch 1, **puff st**—*see Pattern Stitche*s); ch 1; *in next ch-1 sp work (puff st, ch 1, puff st); ch 1; rep from * 10 times more; join in top of first puff st—*24 puff sts*. Finish off Color B.

Rnd 3: Join Color C in any ch-1 sp; ch 6 *(counts as a tr and a ch-2 sp)*, tr in same sp—*beg corner made*; ch 1, dc in next ch-1 sp, [ch 1, hdc in next ch-1 sp] 3 times; ch 1, dc in next ch-1 sp, ch 1; *in next ch-1 sp work (tr, ch 2, tr)—*corner made*; ch 1, dc in next ch-1 sp, [ch 1, hdc in next ch-1 sp] 3 times; ch 1, dc in next ch-1 sp, ch 1; rep from * twice more; join in 4th ch of beg ch-6.

Rnd 4: Sl st in next ch-2 sp, ch 1, in same sp work (sc, ch 1, sc)—*sc corner made*; [ch 1, sc in next ch-1 sp] 6 times; ch 1; *in next corner ch-2 sp work (sc, ch 1, sc)—*sc corner made*; [ch 1, sc in next ch-1 sp] 6 times; ch 1; rep from * twice more; join in first sc.

Finish off and weave in all ends. ●

Square 46

Materials

- Yarn—Color A gold; Color B dark blue

Instructions

With Color A, ch 4; join to form a ring.

Rnd 1 (RS): Ch 4 *(counts as a tr)*, 23 tr in ring; join in 4th ch of beg ch-4—*24 tr.*

Rnd 2: Ch 1, sc in same ch; *ch 6, sc in 2nd ch from hook, hdc in next ch, dc in next 3 chs—*point made*; sk next 2 tr, sc in next tr; rep from * 7 times more, ending last rep without working last sc; join in first sc—*8 points*. Finish off Color A.

Rnd 3: Join Color B in skipped ch at tip of any point; ch 1, in same ch work (sc, ch 1, sc); *working in back lps only on same point, hdc in next sc, dc in next hdc, tr in next dc, sk next 2 dc and next sc; working in unused lps of ch on next point, sk next 2 lps, tr in next lp, dc in next lp, hdc in next lp**; in skipped ch at tip of point work (sc, ch 1, sc); rep from * 6 times more, then rep from * to ** once; join in first sc.

Rnd 4: Sl st in next ch-1 sp and in next sc; ch 2 *(counts as an hdc)*, dc in next 2 sts, 2 tr in next tr; ch 2, 2 tr in next tr—*corner made*; *dc in next 2 sts, hdc in next sc, sk next ch-1 sp, sc in next 8 sts, sk next ch-1 sp, hdc in next sc, dc in next 2 sts, 2 tr in next tr; ch 2, 2 tr in next tr—*corner made*; rep from * twice more; dc in next 2 sts, hdc in next sc, sk next ch-1 sp, sc in next 8 sts, sk next ch-1 sp; join in 2nd ch of beg ch-2.

Rnd 5: Ch 1, sc in same ch and in next 4 sts; 3 sc in next corner ch-2 sp—*sc corner made*; *sc in next 18 sts, 3 sc in next corner ch-2 sp—*sc corner made*; rep from * twice more; sc in next 13 sts; join in first sc.

Finish off and weave in all ends. ●

Square 47

Materials
• Yarn—Color light turquoise

Pattern Stitches

Beginning Cluster (beg CL): Ch 2, keeping last lp of each dc on hook, 2 dc in sp indicated; yo and draw through all 3 lps on hook—*beg CL made.*

Cluster (CL): Keeping last lp of each dc on hook, 3 dc in sp indicated; yo and draw through all 4 lps on hook—*CL made.*

Instructions
Ch 7.

Rnd 1 (RS): In 7th ch from hook work [dc, ch 3] 3 times *(6 skipped chs count as a dc and a ch-3 sp)*; join in 3rd ch of beg 6 skipped chs—*4 dc.*

Rnd 2: Ch 1, sc in same ch; in next ch-3 sp work (dc, 5 tr, dc)—*shell made*; *sc in next dc, in next ch-3 sp work (dc, 5 tr, dc)—*shell made*; rep from * twice more; join in first sc—*4 shells.*

Rnd 3: Ch 1, sc in same sc; *dc in next dc, 2 dc in each of next 2 tr; 3 dc in next tr; 2 dc in each of next 2 tr; dc in next dc**; sc in next sc; rep from * twice more, then rep from * to ** once; join in first sc.

Rnd 4: Sl st in next 4 dc, ch 1, sc in same dc; *ch 5, sk next 5 dc, sc in next dc, ch 5, sk next 7 sts**; sc in next dc; rep from * twice more, then rep from * to ** once; join in first sc—*8 ch-5 sps.*

Rnd 5: Sl st in next ch-5-sp, in same sp work (**beg CL**—*see Pattern Stitches*, ch 3, **CL**—*see Pattern Stitches*)—*beg corner made*; ch 2, 7 dc in next ch-5 sp; ch 2; *in next ch-5 sp work (CL, ch 3, CL)—*corner made*; ch 2, 7 dc in next ch-5 sp; ch 2; rep from * twice more; join in top of beg CL.

Rnd 6: Sl st in next ch-3 sp, beg corner in same sp; ch 2, 3 dc in next ch-2 sp; dc in next 7 dc, 3 dc in next ch-2 sp; ch 2; *in next corner ch-3 sp work corner; ch 2, 3 dc in next ch-2 sp; dc in next 7 dc, 3 dc in next ch-2 sp; ch 2; rep from * twice more; join in top of beg CL.

Rnd 7: Sl st in next ch-3 sp, beg corner in same sp; ch 2, 2 dc in next ch-2 sp; dc in next 13 dc, 2 dc in next ch-2 sp; ch 2; *corner in next corner; ch 2, 2 dc in next ch-2 sp; dc in next 13 dc, 2 dc in next ch-2 sp; ch 2; rep from * twice more; join in top of beg CL.

Rnd 8: Ch 1, sc in same CL; 3 sc in next ch-3 sp—*sc corner made*; sc in next CL, 2 sc in next ch-2 sp; sc in next 17 dc, 2 sc in next ch-2 sp; *sc in next CL, 3 sc in next corner ch-3 sp—*sc corner made*; sc in next CL, 2 sc in next ch-2 sp; sc in next 17 dc, 2 sc in next ch-2 sp; rep from * twice more; join in first sc.

Finish off and weave in ends. ●

Square 48

Materials
• Yarn—Color red

Instructions
Ch 3, join to form a ring.

Row 1 (WS): Ch 1, 3 sc in ring. Ch 1, turn.

Row 2 (RS): Sc in next sc, 3 sc in next sc; sc in next sc—*5 sc*. Ch 1, turn.

Row 3: Sc in next 2 sc, 3 sc in next sc; sc in next 2 sc—*7 sc*. Ch 1, turn.

Row 4: Sc in next 3 sc, 3 sc in next sc; sc in next 3 sc—*9 sc*. Ch 1, turn.

Row 5: Sc in next 4 sc, 3 sc in next sc; sc in next 4 sc—*11 sc*. Ch 1, turn.

Row 6: Sc in next 5 sc, 3 sc in next sc; sc in next 5 sc—*13 sc*. Ch 1, turn.

Row 7: Sc in next 6 sc, 3 sc in next sc; sc in next 6 sc—*15 sc*. Ch 1, turn.

Row 8: Sc in next 7 sc, 3 sc in next sc; sc in next 7 sc—*17 sc*. Ch 4 *(counts as first dc and ch-1 sp on following rows)*, turn.

Row 9: Sk next sc, dc in next sc, [ch 1, sk next sc, dc in next sc] twice; ch 1, sk next sc, in next sc work (dc, ch 3, dc); [ch 1, sk next sc, dc in next sc] 4 times. Ch 1, turn.

Row 10: Working in each dc and in each ch-1 sp, sc in next 9 sts, 5 sc in next ch-3 sp; sc in next 7 sts, in turning ch-4 sp, and in 3rd ch of same turning ch-4. Ch 4, turn.

Row 11: Sk next sc, dc in next sc, [ch 1, sk next sc, dc in next sc] 4 times; ch 1, in next sc work (dc, ch 3, dc); ch 1, dc in next sc, [ch 1, sk next sc, dc in next sc] 5 times—*6 ch-1 sps on each side*. Ch 1, turn.

Row 12: Working in each dc and in each ch-1 sp, sc in next 13 sts, 5 sc in next ch-3 sp; sc in next 11 sts, in turning ch-4 sp, and in 3rd ch of same turning ch-4. Ch 4, turn.

Row 13: Sk next sc, dc in next sc, [ch 1, sk next sc, dc in next sc] 6 times; ch 1, in next sc work (dc, ch 3, dc); ch 1, dc in next sc, [ch 1, sk next sc, dc in next sc] 7 times—*8 ch-1 sps on each side*. Ch 1, turn.

Row 14: Working in each dc and in each ch-1 sp, sc in next 17 sts, 5 sc in next ch-3 sp; sc in next 15 sts, in next turning ch-4 sp, and in 3rd ch of same turning ch-4. Ch 4, turn.

Row 15: Sk next sc, dc in next sc, [ch 1, sk next sc, dc in next sc] 8 times; ch 1, in next sc work (dc, ch 3, dc); ch 1, dc in next sc, [ch 1, sk next sc, dc in next sc] 9 times—*10 ch-1 sps on each side*. Ch 1, turn.

Border: Working in each dc and in each ch-1 sp, sc in next 21 sts, 3 sc in next ch-3 sp—*corner made*; sc in next 19 sts, in next turning ch-4 sp, and in 3rd ch of turning ch-4; working along next side in ends of sc rows and in sps formed by edge dc, 3 sc in sp formed by same turning ch-4—*corner made*; [sc in side of next row, 2 sc in next sp] 3 times; sc in side of each of next 8 rows, 3 sc in beg ring—*corner made*; working along next side, sc in side of next 8 rows, [2 sc in next sp, sc in side of next row] 3 times; 3 sc in next sp—*corner made*; join in first sc.

Finish off and weave in ends. ●

Square 49

Materials
- Yarn—Color A dark pink; Color B off white; Color C spring green; Color D black

Instructions
With Color A, ch 2.

Rnd 1 (RS): 8 sc in 2nd ch from hook; join in first sc.

Rnd 2: Ch 3 *(counts as a dc on this and following rnds)*, dc in same sc; 2 dc in each rem sc; join in 3rd ch of beg ch-3—*16 dc*.

Rnd 3: Ch 3, dc in same ch; 3 dc in next dc; [2 dc in next dc, 3 dc in next dc] 7 times; join in 3rd ch of beg ch-3—*40 dc*. Change to Color B by drawing lp through; cut Color A.

Rnd 4: Ch 1, sc in same ch as joining and in each dc; join in first sc. Change to Color C by drawing lp through; cut Color B.

Rnd 5: Ch 1, sc in same sc; 2 sc in next sc; [sc in next sc, 2 sc in next sc] 19 times; join in first sc—*60 sc*. Change to Color B by drawing lp through; cut Color C.

Rnd 6: Ch 2 *(counts as an hdc)*, hdc in next 3 sc, sc in next 8 sc, [hdc in next 7 sc, sc in next 8 sc] 3 times; hdc in next 3 sc; join in 2nd ch of beg ch-2.

Rnd 7: Ch 7 *(counts as a tr and a ch-3 sp)*, tr in same sc—*beg corner made*; *dc in next 3 sts, hdc in next 2 sts, sc in next 4 sc, hdc in next 2 sts, dc in next 3 sts, in next sc work (tr, ch 3, tr)—*corner made*; rep from * twice more; dc in next 3 sts, hdc in next 2 sts, sc in next 4 sc, hdc in next 2 sts, dc in next 3 sts; join in 4th ch of beg ch-7.

Finish off and weave in all ends.

Seeds
Thread tapestry needle with Color D. Referring to photo for placement, work 8 Lazy Daisy stitches (*see illustration*), over Rnd 2.

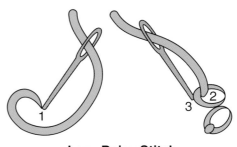

Lazy Daisy Stitch

Thread tapestry needle with Color D. Bring yarn up at A, loop yarn, insert needle in same hole, and bring it up at loop end. Pull needle through, adjust loop, and take a small stitch down over loop to secure. ●

Square 50

Materials
- Yarn—Color A dark pink; Color B light pink

Pattern Stitch

Puff Stitch (puff st): Yo, insert hook in indicated st, yo, pull lp through st and make lp same height as previous sts in working row, (yo, insert hook in same st, yo, pull lp through st and make lp same height as working row) twice, yo, pull through all 7 lps on hook—*puff st made.*

Instructions

Square
With Color A, ch 8; join to form a ring.

Rnd 1 (RS): Ch 1, [**puff st** *(see Pattern Stitch)* in ring, ch 2] 8 times; join in top of first puff sts—*8 puff sts.* Change to Color B by drawing lp through; cut Color A.

Rnd 2: Ch 6 *(counts as a dc and a ch-3 sp),* dc in same puff st—*beg corner made;* ch 2, puff st in next ch-2 sp; ch 2, puff st in next puff st; ch 2, puff st in next ch-2 sp; ch 2; *in next puff st work (dc, ch 3, dc)—*corner made;* ch 2, puff st in next ch-2 sp; ch 2, puff st in next puff st; ch 2, puff st in next ch-2 sp; ch 2; rep from * twice more; join in 3rd ch of beg ch-6—*12 puff sts.*

Rnd 3: Sl st in next ch-3 sp, beg corner in same sp; ch 2; *[puff st in next ch-2 sp, ch 2] 4 times; in next corner ch-3 sp work corner, ch 2; rep from * twice more; [puff st in next ch-2 sp, ch 2] 4 times; join in 3rd ch of beg ch-6—*16 puff sts.*

Rnd 4: Sl st in next ch-3 sp, beg corner in same sp; ch 2, in each ch-2 sp to next corner ch-3 sp work (puff st, ch 2); *corner in next corner; ch 2, in each ch-2 sp to next corner ch-3 sp work (puff st, ch 2); rep from * twice more; join in 3rd ch of beg ch-6.

Rnds 5 and 6: Rep Rnd 4. At end of Rnd 6, finish off Color B.

Rnd 7: Join Color A in any corner ch-3 sp; ch 1, 5 sc in same sp—*sc corner made;* *3 sc in each of next 8 ch-2 sps; 5 sc in next corner ch-3 sp—*sc corner made;* rep from * twice more; 3 sc in each of next 8 ch-2 sps; join in first sc. Finish off Color A.

Petals

Hold Square with right side facing you; join Color A in any ch-2 sp on Rnd 1 (beside puff st on Rnd 2); ch 1, in same sp work (sc, ch 1, puff st, ch 1, puff st, ch 1, sc)—*petal made;* in each rem ch-2 sp work (sc, ch 1, puff st, ch 1, puff st, ch 1, sc)—*petal made;* join in first sc—*8 petals.*

Finish off and weave in all ends. ●

Square 51

Materials
- Yarn—Color A yellow; Color B dark blue

Pattern Stitch
Long Double Crochet (long dc): Yo, insert hook in st indicated on 2nd rnd below, draw up lp to height of working rnd, [yo, draw through 2 lps on hook] twice—long *dc made*.

Instructions
With Color A, ch 4; join to form a ring.

Rnd 1 (RS): Ch 1, 6 sc in ring; join in first sc.

Rnd 2: Ch 1, 2 sc in each sc; join in first sc—*12 sc*.

Rnd 3: Rep Rnd 2. At end of rnd—*24 sc*.

Rnd 4: Ch 2, yo, draw up lp in same sc, yo and draw through all 3 lps on hook—*beg cluster made*; ch 2; *sk next sc, yo, draw up lp in next sc, yo, draw through 2 lps on hook, yo and draw up lp in same sc, yo and draw through all 4 lps on hook—*cluster made*; ch 2; rep from * 10 times more; join in top of beg cluster—*12 clusters*. Change to Color B by drawing lp through; cut Color A.

Rnd 5: Ch 1, sc in same cluster; working over next ch-2 sp, **long dc** (see Pattern Stitch) in unused sc on 2nd rnd below; long dc as before in same sc; *sc in top of next cluster on working rnd, working over next ch-2 sp, 2 long dc in next unused sc on 2nd rnd below; rep from * 10 times more; join in first sc—*36 sts*.

Rnd 6: Ch 1, 2 sc in same sc; sc in next 2 dc, [2 sc in next sc, sc in next 2 dc] 11 times; join in first sc—*48 sc*.

Rnd 7: Ch 6 (counts as a dc and a ch-3 sp), dc in same sc—*beg corner made*; hdc in next 2 sc, sc in next 7 sc, hdc in next 2 sc; *in next sc work (dc, ch 3, dc)—*corner made*; hdc in next 2 sc, sc in next 7 sc, hdc in next 2 sc; rep from * twice more; join in 3rd ch of beg ch-6.

Finish off and weave in all ends. ●

Square 52

Materials
- Yarn—Color A light yellow; Color B blue

Instructions
With Color A, ch 6; join to form a ring.

Rnd 1 (RS): Ch 3 *(counts as a dc on this and following rnds)*, 15 dc in ring; join in 3rd ch of beg ch-3—*16 dc.*

Rnd 2: Ch 4 *(counts as a dc and a ch-1 sp)*, [dc in next dc, ch 1] 15 times; join in 3rd ch of beg ch-4.

Rnd 3: Ch 3, 2 dc in next ch-1 sp; [dc in next dc, 2 dc in next ch-1 sp] 15 times; join in 3rd ch of beg ch-3—*48 dc.* Change to Color B by drawing lp through; cut Color A.

Rnd 4: Ch 1, sc in same ch; *ch 5, sl st in 5th ch from hook; sk next 2 dc, sc in next dc, ch 2, sk next 2 dc, sc in next dc, ch 3, sk next 2 dc, sc in next dc, ch 2, sk next 2 dc, sc in next dc; rep from * twice more; ch 5, sl st in 5th ch from hook; sk next 2 dc, sc in next dc, ch 2, sk next 2 dc, sc in next dc, ch 3, sk next 2 dc, sc in next dc, ch 2, sk next 2 dc; join in first sc.

Rnd 5: Sl st in next ch-5 sp, ch 3, in same sp work (4 dc, ch 3, 5 dc)—*beg corner made*; sc in next ch-2 sp, 5 dc in next ch-3 sp; sc in next ch-2 sp; * in next ch-5 sp work (5 dc, ch 3, 5 dc)—*corner made*; sc in next ch-2 sp, 5 dc in next ch-3 sp; sc in next ch-2 sp; rep from * twice more; join in 3rd ch of beg ch-3. Finish off Color B.

Rnd 6: Join Color A in any corner ch-3 sp; ch 1, in same sp work (sc, ch 3, sc)—*sc corner made*; ch 5, dc in next sc, ch 3, sk next 2 dc, sc in next dc, ch 3, sk next 2 dc, dc in next sc, ch 5; *in next ch-3 sp work (sc, ch 3, sc)—*sc corner made*; ch 5, dc in next sc, ch 3, sk next 2 dc, sc in next dc, ch 3, sk next 2 dc, dc in next sc, ch 5; rep from * twice more; join in first sc.

Rnd 7: Sl st in next ch-3 sp, ch 1, 5 sc in same ch-3 sp—*5-sc corner made*; 5 sc in next ch-5 sp; 3 sc in each of next 2 ch-3 sps; 5 sc in next ch-5 sp; * 5 sc in next corner ch-3 sp—*5-sc corner made*; 5 sc in next ch-5 sp; 3 sc in each of next 2 ch-3 sps; 5 sc in next ch-5 sp; rep from * twice more; join in first sc.

Finish off and weave in all ends. ●

Square 53

Materials
- Yarn—Color A red; Color B yellow; Color C turquoise

Pattern Stitch

Beginning Cluster (beg CL): Ch 2, keeping last lp of each dc on hook, 2 dc in sp indicated; yo and draw through all 3 lps on hook—*beg CL made*.

Cluster (CL): Keeping last lp of each dc on hook, 3 dc in sp indicated; yo and draw through all 4 lps on hook—*CL made*.

Instructions
With Color A, ch 6; join to form a ring.

Rnd 1 (RS): Beg CL *(see Pattern Stitches)* in ring; ch 3, [**CL** *(see Pattern Stitches)* in ring, ch 3] 7 times; join in top of beg CL—*8 CLs*. Finish off Color A.

Rnd 2: Join Color B in any ch-3 sp; in same sp work (beg CL, ch 3, CL)—*shell made*; ch 3; *in next ch-3 sp work (CL, ch 3, CL)—*shell made*; ch 3; rep from * 6 times more; join in top of beg CL—*8 shells*. Finish off Color B.

Rnd 3: Join Color C in ch-3 sp of any shell; ch 3 *(counts as a dc on this and following rnds)*, in same sp work (2 dc, ch 3, 3 dc)—*beg corner made*; ch 1, 3 dc in ch-3 sp of next shell; ch 1; *in ch-3 sp of next shell work (3 dc, ch 3, 3 dc)—*corner made*; ch 1, 3 dc in ch-3 sp of next shell; ch 1; rep from * twice more; join in 3rd ch of beg ch-3.

Rnd 4: Sl st in next 2 dc and in next ch-3 sp, beg corner in same sp; ch 1, [3 dc in next ch-1 sp, ch 1] twice; *in next corner ch-3 sp work corner; ch 1, [3 dc in next ch-1 sp, ch 1] twice; rep from * twice more; join in 3rd ch of beg ch-3.

Rnd 5: Sl st in next 2 dc and in next ch-3 sp, beg corner in same sp; ch 1, [3 dc in next ch-1 sp, ch 1] 3 times; *corner in next corner; ch 1, [3 dc in next ch-1 sp, ch 1] 3 times; rep from * twice more; join in 3rd ch of beg ch-3.

Rnd 6: Ch 1, sc in same ch as joining and in next 2 dc; 3 sc in next corner ch-3 sp—*sc corner made*; *working in each dc and in each ch, sc in next 19 sts, 3 sc in next corner ch-3 sp—*sc corner made*; rep from * twice more; sc in next 16 sts; join in first sc.

Finish off and weave in all ends. ●

Square 54

Materials
- Yarn—Color turquoise

Instructions
Ch 8, join to form a ring.

Rnd 1 (RS): Ch 3, tr in ring—*beg cluster made*; ch 1; *keeping last lp of each tr on hook, 2 tr in ring; yo and draw through all 3 lps on hook—*cluster made*; ch 1; rep from * 14 times more; join in top of beg cluster—*16 clusters*.

Rnd 2: Sl st in next ch-1 sp, ch 3 *(counts as a dc on this and following rnds)*, in same sp work (dc, ch 2, 2 dc)—*beg corner made*; ch 3, [sc in next ch-1 sp, ch 3] 3 times; *in next ch-1 sp work (2 dc, ch 2, 2 dc)—*corner made*; ch 3, [sc in next ch-1 sp, ch 3] 3 times; rep from * twice more; join in 3rd ch of beg ch-3.

Rnd 3: Sl st in next dc and in next ch-2 sp, ch 3, in same sp work (2 dc, ch 3, 3 dc)—**beg 3-dc corner made**; ch 2, sk next ch-3 sp, [3 dc in next ch-3 sp, ch 2] twice; sk next ch-3 sp; * in next ch-2 sp work (3 dc, ch 3, 3 dc)—*3-dc corner made*; ch 2, sk next ch-3 sp,

[3 dc in next ch-3 sp, ch 2] twice; sk next ch-3 sp; rep from * twice more; join in 3rd ch of beg ch-3.

Rnd 4: Sl st in next 2 dc and in next ch-3 sp, beg 3-dc corner in same sp; ch 2, [3 dc in next ch-2 sp, ch 2] 3 times; *in next corner ch-3 sp work 3-dc corner; ch 2, [3 dc in next ch-2 sp, ch 2] 3 times; rep from * twice more; join in 3rd ch of beg ch-3.

Rnd 5: Sl st in next 2 dc and in next ch-3 sp, beg 3-dc corner in same sp; 3 dc in each of next 4 ch-2 sps; *3-dc corner in next corner; 3 dc in each of next 4 ch-2 sps; rep from * twice more; join in 3rd ch of beg ch-3.

Rnd 6: Ch 1, sc in same ch as joining and in next 2 dc; 3 sc in next corner ch-3 sp—*sc corner made*; *sc in next 18 dc, 3 sc in next corner ch-3 sp—*sc corner made*; rep from * twice more; sc in next 15 dc; join in first sc.

Finish off and weave in ends. ●

Square 55

Materials
- Yarn—Color light purple

Instructions

Ch 18.

Row 1 (RS): Dc in 6th ch from hook, [ch 1, sk next ch, dc in next ch] 6 times. Ch 4 *(counts as first dc and ch-1 sp on following rows)*, turn.

Row 2: Dc in next dc, [ch 1, sk next ch-1 sp, dc in next dc] 5 times; ch 1, sk next ch, dc in next ch. Ch 4, turn.

Row 3: Dc in next dc, [ch 1, sk next ch-1 sp, dc in next dc] 5 times; ch 1, sk next ch, dc in next ch. Ch 4, turn.

Rows 4–7: Rep Row 3. At end of Row 7, do not ch 4; do not turn.

Note: Remainder of square is worked in rnds.

Rnd 1: Working along next side in sps formed by edge dc and turning chs, in next sp work (sl st, ch 1, 2 sc); *2 sc in each of next 2 sps; in next sp work (sc, ch 4, sc); 2 sc in each of next 2 sps**; in next sp work (2 sc, ch 1, 2 sc)—*corner made*; working along next side in sps formed by unused chs of beg ch, 2 sc in each of next 2 sps; in next sp work (sc, ch 4, sc); 2 sc in each of next 2 sps; in next sp work (2 sc, ch 1, 2 sc)—*corner made*; working along next side in sps formed by edge dc and turning chs, rep from * to ** once; in next sp work (2 sc, ch 1, 2 sc)—*corner made*; working across Row 7, 2 sc in each of next 2 ch-1 sps; in next ch-1 sp work (sc, ch 4, sc); 2 sc in each of next 2 ch-1 sps; 2 sc in next ch-1 sp; ch 1; join in first sc—*beg corner made*.

Rnd 2: Loosely sl st in next 5 sc; sk next sc, in next ch-4 sp work [sc, ch 3, sl st in 3rd ch from hook—*picot made*] 5 times; sc in same sp; sk next sc, loosely sl st in next 6 sc; *sc in next corner ch-1 sp—*corner sc made*; loosely sl st in next 6 sc; sk next sc, in next ch-4 sp work [sc, ch 3, sl st in 3rd ch from hook—*picot made*] 5 times; sc in same sp; sk next sc, loosely sl st in next 6 sc; rep from * twice more; sc in next corner ch-1 sp—*corner sc made*; join in joining sl st. Finish off.

Rnd 3: Join yarn in any corner sc; ch 1, sc in same sc; ch 5, sk next picot, sl st in next picot; ch 6, sk next picot, sl st in next picot; ch 5; *sc in next corner sc, ch 5, sk next picot, sl st in next picot; ch 6, sk next picot, sl st in next picot; ch 5; rep from * twice more; join in first sc.

Rnd 4: Ch 1, sc in same sc; 5 sc in next ch-5 sp; sc in next sl st, in next ch-6 sp work (4 sc, ch 2, 4 sc)—*4-sc corner made*; sc in next sl st, 5 sc in next ch-5 sp; *sc in next sc, 5 sc in next ch-5 sp; sc in next sl st, in next ch-6 sp work (4 sc, ch 2, 4 sc)—*4-sc corner made*; sc in next sl st, 5 sc in next ch-5 sp; rep from * twice more; join in first sc.

Rnd 5: Ch 1, sc in same sc and in next 10 sc; in next corner ch-2 sp work (sc, ch 2, sc)—*ch-2 corner made*; *sc in next 21 sc, in next corner ch-2 sp work (sc, ch 2, sc)—*ch-2 corner made*; rep from * twice more; sc in next 10 sc; join in first sc. Finish off.

Rnd 6: Join yarn in any corner ch-2 sp; ch 5 *(counts as a dc and ch-2 sp)*, dc in same ch—*beg dc corner made*; ch 1, [sk next sc, dc in next sc, ch 1] 11 times; *in next corner ch-2 sp work (dc, ch 2, dc)—*dc corner made*; ch 1, [sk next sc, dc in next sc, ch 1] 11 times; rep from * twice more; join in 3rd ch of beg ch-5.

Rnd 7: Ch 1, sc in same ch as joining; 3 sc in next corner ch-2 sp—*3-sc corner made*; *working in each dc and ch-1 sp, sc in next 25 sts, 3 sc in next corner ch-2 sp—*3-sc corner made*; rep from * twice more; sc in next 24 sts; join in first sc.

Finish off and weave in all ends. ●

Square 56

Materials
- Yarn—Color pink

Pattern Stitches

Popcorn (PC): 5 dc in ring or st indicated; drop lp from hook, insert hook in first dc made, draw dropped lp through—*PC made.*

Beginning Cluster (beg CL): Ch 2, keeping last lp of each dc on hook; 2 dc in st indicated; yo and draw through all 3 lps on hook—*beg CL made.*

Cluster (CL): Keeping last lp of each dc on hook, 3 dc in st indicated; yo and draw through all 4 lps on hook—*CL made.*

Instructions

Ch 8, join to form a ring.

Rnd 1: Ch 3 *(counts as a dc on this and following rnds)*, **PC** *(see Pattern Stitches)* in ring; in ring work (dc, PC) 7 times; join in 3rd ch of beg ch-3—*8 PCs.*

Rnd 2: In same ch work (**beg CL**—*see Pattern Stitches, ch 2, **CL**—see Pattern Stitches)—*beg corner made*; ch 1, sk next PC, 3 dc in next dc; ch 1, sk next PC; *in next dc work (CL, ch 2, CL)—*corner made*; ch 1, sk next PC, 3 dc in next dc; ch 1, sk next PC; rep from * twice more; join in top of beg CL.

Rnd 3: Sl st in next ch-2 sp, beg corner in same sp; ch 1, 2 dc in next ch-1 sp; dc in next 3 dc, 2 dc in next ch-1 sp; ch 1; *in next corner ch-2 sp work corner; ch 1, 2 dc in next ch-1 sp; dc in next 3 dc, 2 dc in next ch-1 sp; ch 1; rep from * twice more; join in top of beg CL.

Rnd 4: Sl st in next ch-2 sp, beg corner in same sp; ch 1, 2 dc in next ch-1 sp; dc in next 3 dc, PC in next dc; dc in next 3 dc, 2 dc in next ch-1 sp; ch 1; *corner in next corner; ch 1, 2 dc in next ch-1 sp; dc in next 3 dc, PC in next dc; dc in next 3 dc, 2 dc in next ch-1 sp; ch 1; rep from * twice more; join in top of beg CL.

Rnd 5: Sl st in next ch-2 sp, beg corner in same sp; ch 1, 2 dc in next ch-1 sp; dc in next 3 dc, PC in next dc; dc in next dc, in next PC, and in next dc; PC in next dc; dc in next 3 dc, 2 dc in next ch-1 sp; ch 1; *corner in next corner; ch 1, 2 dc in next ch-1 sp; dc in next 3 dc, PC in next dc; dc in next dc, in next PC, and in next dc; PC in next dc; dc in next 3 dc, 2 dc in next ch-1 sp; rep from * twice more; join in top of beg CL.

Rnd 6: Sl st in next ch-2 sp, beg corner in same sp; ch 1, 2 dc in next ch-1 sp; dc in next 3 dc, PC in next dc; [dc in next dc, in next PC, and in next dc; PC in next dc] twice; dc in next 3 dc, 2 dc in next ch-1 sp; ch 1; *corner in next corner; ch 1, 2 dc in next ch-1 sp; dc in next 3 dc, PC in next dc; [dc in next dc, in next PC, and in next dc; PC in next dc] twice; dc in next 3 dc, 2 dc in next ch-1 sp; rep from * twice more; join in top of beg CL.

Finish off and weave in ends. ●

Square 57

Materials
• Yarn—Color A dark pink; Color B spring green

Instructions
With Color A, ch 4; join to form a ring.

Rnd 1 (RS): Ch 3 *(counts as a dc on this and following rnds)*, 15 dc in ring; join in 3rd ch of beg ch-3—*16 dc*. Finish off Color A.

Rnd 2: Join Color B in sp between any 2 dc; ch 3, dc in same sp; working in sps between dc, 2 dc in each rem sp; join in 3rd ch of beg ch-3—*32 dc*. Change to Color A by drawing lp through; cut Color B.

Rnd 3: Ch 2 *(counts as an hdc)*, hdc in same ch; working in back lps only, hdc in next dc, [2 hdc in next dc, hdc in next dc] 15 times; join in 2nd ch of beg ch-2—*48 hdc*. Change to Color B by drawing lp through; cut Color A.

Rnd 4: Ch 4 *(counts as a tr)*, in same ch work (2 dc, ch 2, 2 dc, tr)—*beg corner made*; sk next 2 hdc, hdc in next 2 hdc, sc in next 3 hdc, hdc in next 2 hdc, sk next 2 hdc; *in next hdc work (tr, 2 dc, ch 2, 2 dc, tr)—corner made*; sk next 2 hdc, hdc in next 2 hdc, sc in next 3 hdc, hdc in next 2 hdc, sk next 2 hdc; rep from * twice more; join in 4th ch of beg ch-4.

Finish off and weave in all ends. ●

Square 58

Materials
• Yarn—Color pink

Pattern Stitches
Beginning Cluster (beg CL): Ch 3, keeping last lp of each tr on hook, 3 tr in sp indicated; yo and draw through all 4 lps on hook—*beg CL made*.

Cluster (CL): Keeping last lp of each tr on hook, 4 tr in sp indicated; yo and draw through all 5 lps on hook—*CL made*.

Instructions
Ch 8, join to form a ring.

Rnd 1 (RS): Ch 4 (counts as a dc and a ch-1 sp), [dc in ring, ch 1] 7 times; join in 3rd ch of beg ch-4—8 dc.

Rnd 2: Sl st in next ch-1 sp, **beg CL** (see Pattern Stitches) in same sp; ch 4; *CL (see Pattern Stitches) in next ch-1 sp, ch 4; rep from * 6 times more; join in top of beg CL—8 CLs.

Rnd 3: Ch 1, sc in same CL; ch 3, dc in next ch-4 sp, ch 3, sc in top of next CL, ch 4; *sc in top of next CL, ch 3, dc in next ch-4 sp, ch 3, sc in top of next CL, ch 4; rep from * twice more; join in first sc.

Rnd 4: Ch 1, sc in same sc; 3 sc in next ch-3 sp; 3 sc in next dc—corner made; 3 sc in next ch-3 sp; sc in next sc, 4 sc in next ch-4 sp; *sc in next sc, 3 sc in next ch-3 sp; 3 sc in next dc—corner made; 3 sc in next ch-3 sp; sc in next sc, 4 sc in next ch-4 sp; rep from * twice more; join in first sc.

Finish off and weave in ends. ●

Square 59

Materials
- Yarn—Color A light pink; Color B purple

Pattern Stitches
Beginning Cluster (beg CL): Ch 2, keeping last lp of each dc on hook, 2 dc in sp indicated; yo and draw through all 3 lps on hook—beg CL made.

Cluster (CL): Keeping last lp of each dc on hook, 3 dc in sp indicated; yo and draw through all 4 lps on hook—CL made.

Instructions
With Color A, ch 5; join to form a ring.

Rnd 1 (RS): Ch 1, 12 sc in ring; join in first sc. Change to Color B by drawing lp through; cut Color A.

Rnd 2: Ch 4 (counts as a dc and a ch-1 sp), [dc in next sc, ch 1] 11 times; join in 3rd ch of beg ch-4—12 dc. Finish off Color B.

Rnd 3: Join Color A in any ch-1 sp; **beg CL** (see Pattern Stitches) in same sp; ch 3; *CL (see Pattern Stitches) in next ch-1 sp; ch 3; rep from * 10 times more; join in top of beg CL—12 CLs. Finish off Color A.

Rnd 4: Join Color B in any ch-3 sp; ch 1, 4 sc in same sp and in each rem ch-3 sp; join in first sc. Change to Color A by drawing lp through; cut Color B.

Rnd 5: Ch 3 (counts as a dc on this and following rnd), in same sc work (dc, ch 2, 2 dc)—beg corner made; ch 2, sk next 2 sc, sc in next 2 sc, ch 3, sk next 3 sc, sc in next 2 sc, ch 2, sk next 2 sc; * in next sc work (2 dc, ch 2, 2 dc)—corner made; ch 2, sk next 2 sc, sc in next 2 sc, ch 3, sk next 3 sc, sc in next 2 sc, ch 2, sk next 2 sc; rep from * twice more; join in 3rd ch of beg ch-3.

Rnd 6: Ch 3, dc in next dc, in next corner ch-2 sp work corner; *working in each dc and in each ch, dc in next 15 sts, in next corner ch-2 sp work corner; rep from * twice more; dc in next 13 sts; join in 3rd ch of beg ch-3.

Finish off and weave in all ends. ●

Square 60

Materials
- Yarn—Color A light pink; Color B dark pink

Instructions
With Color A, ch 8; join to form a ring.

Rnd 1 (RS): Ch 3 *(counts as a dc on this and following rnds)*, 3 dc in ring; ch 2, [4 dc in ring, ch 2] 7 times; join in 3rd ch of beg ch-3—*8 4-dc groups*. Finish off Color A.

Rnd 2: Join Color B in any ch-2 sp; ch 3, in same sp work (2 dc, ch 3, 3 dc); ch 1; *in next ch-2 sp work (3 dc, ch 3, 3 dc); ch 1; rep from * 6 times more; join in 3rd ch of beg ch-3. Finish off Color B.

Rnd 3: Join Color A in any ch-1 sp; ch 1, sc in same sp; 9 dc in next ch-3 sp; [sc in next ch-1 sp, 9 dc in next ch-3 sp] 7 times; join in first sc. Finish off Color A.

Rnd 4: Join Color B in 5th dc of any 9-dc group; ch 1, sc in same dc; ch 2, dc in next sc, ch 2, sc in 5th dc of next 9-dc group, ch 2; *in next sc work (3 tr, ch 3, 3 tr)—*corner made*; ch 2, sc in 5th dc of next 9-dc group, ch 2, dc in next sc, ch 2, sc in 5th dc of

next 9-dc group, ch 2; rep from * twice more; in next sc work (3 tr, ch 3, 3 tr)—*corner made*; ch 2; join in first sc.

Rnd 5: Ch 1, sc in same sc; 2 sc in next ch-2 sp; sc in next dc, 2 sc in next ch-2 sp; sc in next sc, 2 sc in next ch-2 sp; hdc in next 3 tr; *in next corner ch-3 sp work (3 dc, ch 2, 3 dc)—*dc corner made*; hdc in next 3 tr, 2 sc in next ch-2 sp; sc in next sc, 2 sc in next ch-2 sp; sc in next dc, 2 sc in next ch-2 sp; sc in next sc, 2 sc in next ch-2 sp; hdc in next 3 tr; rep from * twice more; in next corner ch-3 sp work (3 dc, ch 2, 3 dc)—*dc corner made*; hdc in next 3 tr, 2 sc in next ch-2 sp; join in first sc.

Rnd 6: Ch 1, sc in same sc and in next 14 sts; *3 sc in next corner ch-2 sp—*sc corner made*; sc in next 23 sts; rep from * twice more; 3 sc in next corner ch-2 sp—*sc corner made*; sc in next 8 sts; join in first sc.

Finish off and weave in all ends. ●

Square 61

Materials
- Yarn—Color red

Pattern Stitches

Beginning Cluster (beg CL): Ch 2, keeping last lp of each dc on hook, 2 dc in sp indicated; yo and draw through all 3 lps on hook—*beg CL made.*

Cluster (CL): Keeping last lp of each dc on hook, 3 dc in sp indicated; yo and draw through all 4 lps on hook—*CL made.*

Instructions

Ch 6, join to form a ring.

Rnd 1 (RS): Ch 3 *(counts as a dc on this and following rnds),* 3 dc in ring; ch 2, [4 dc in ring, ch 2] 3 times; join in 3rd ch of beg ch-3—*16 dc.*

Rnd 2: Sl st in next dc and between same dc and next dc, ch 1, sc in same sp; 9 dc in next ch-2 sp—*corner made;* *sk next dc, sc between next 2 dc; 9 dc in next ch-2 sp—*corner made;* rep from * twice more; join in first sc. Finish off.

Rnd 3: Join yarn between 4th and 5th dc of any corner; ch 1, sc in same sp; ch 2, sc between next 2 dc, ch 2, dc in first dc of next corner, ch 2, working in front of dc just made, dc in last dc of prev corner, ch 2; *sc between 4th and 5th dc of working corner, ch 2, sc between next 2 dc, ch 2, dc in first dc of next corner, ch 2, working in front of dc just made, dc in last dc of prev corner, ch 2; rep from * twice more; join in first sc.

Rnd 4: Sl st in next ch-2 sp, in same sp work (**beg CL**—*see Pattern Stitches,* ch 2, **CL**—*see Pattern Stitches,* ch 3, CL, ch 2, CL)—*beg CL corner made;* ch 3, sk next ch-2 sp, sc in next ch-2 sp, ch 3, sk next ch-2 sp; *in next ch-2 sp work (CL, ch 2, CL, ch 3, CL, ch 2, CL)—*CL corner made;* ch 3, sk next ch-2 sp, sc in next ch-2 sp, ch 3, sk next ch-2 sp; rep from * twice more; join in top of beg CL.

Rnd 5: Ch 1, sc in same CL; working in each ch, in each CL, and in each sc, sc in each rem st; join in first sc.

Finish off and weave in all ends. ●

Square 62

Materials

- Yarn—Color A off white; Color B red; Color C emerald green

Instructions

Square

With Color A, ch 4; join to form a ring.

Rnd 1 (RS): Ch 3 *(counts as a dc on this and following rnds),* 2 dc in ring; ch 3, [3 dc in ring, ch 3] 3 times; join in 3rd ch of beg ch-3—*4 ch-3 sps.*

Rnd 2: Sl st in next 2 dc and in next ch-3 sp, ch 3, in same sp work (2 dc, ch 3, 3 dc)—*corner made;* *in next ch-3 sp work (3 dc, ch 3, 3 dc)—*corner made;* rep from * twice more; join in 3rd ch of beg ch-3.

Rnd 3: Sl st in next 2 dc and in next ch-3 sp, beg corner in same sp; 3 dc between next two 3-dc groups; *in next corner ch-3 sp work corner; 3 dc between next two 3-dc groups; rep from * twice more; join in 3rd ch of beg ch-3.

Rnd 4: Sl st in next 2 dc and in next ch-3 sp, beg corner in same sp; working in sps between 3-dc groups, 3 dc in each of next 2 sps; *corner in next corner; 3 dc in each of next 2 sps; rep from * twice more; join in 3rd ch of beg ch-3.

Rnd 5: Sl st in next 2 dc and in next ch-3 sp, beg corner in same sp; working in sps between 3-dc groups, 3 dc in each of next 3 sps; *corner in next corner; 3 dc in each of next 3 sps; rep from * twice more; join in 3rd ch of beg ch-3. Finish off Color A.

Rnd 6: Join Color B in any corner ch-3 sp; beg corner in same sp; working in sps between 3-dc groups, 3 dc in each of next 4 sps; *corner in next corner; 3 dc in each of next 4 sps; rep from * twice more; join in 3rd ch of beg ch-3.

Finish off and weave in all ends.

Holly Berry

Make 3
With Color B, ch 2.

Note: Berry is worked in continuous rnds; do not join.

Rnd 1: 6 sc in 2nd ch from hook.

Rnd 2: Sc in each sc.

Rnd 3: Rep Rnd 2. Finish off, leaving a 6" end for sewing.

Holly Leaves
Make 3

With Color C, ch 11; beg at tip of leaf and working in top lp of each ch, sl st in 2nd ch from hook; *sc in next ch, hdc in next ch, dc in next ch, ch 3, sl st in 3rd ch from hook; rep from * once more; sc in next ch, sl st in next ch, 3 sl sts in last ch; working along opposite side in bottom lps of beg ch, sl st in next lp, sc in next lp, ch 3, sl st in 3rd ch from hook, sc in next lp, hdc in next lp, dc in next lp, ch 3, sl st in 3rd ch from hook, sc in next lp, sl st in next 3 lps. Finish off, leaving a 6" end for sewing.

Finishing
Referring to photo for placement and with tapestry needle, tack Leaves to Square. For each Berry, thread tapestry needle with 6" yarn end and weave through sts of last rnd. Draw up tightly and secure. Tack to center of Square. ●

Square 63

Materials
- Yarn—Color A yellow; Color B light turquoise; Color C dark turquoise

Instructions
With Color A, ch 5; join to form a ring.

Rnd 1 (RS): Ch 4 *(counts as a tr on this and following rnds)*, tr in ring, ch 2, [2 tr in ring, ch 2] 7 times; join in 4th ch of beg ch-4—*16 tr.* Change to Color B by drawing lp through; cut Color A.

Rnd 2: Ch 3 *(counts as a dc on this and following rnds)*, 2 dc in next tr; ch 2, [dc in next tr, 2 dc in next tr, ch 2] 7 times; join in 3rd ch of beg ch-3—*24 dc.*

Rnd 3: Ch 3, 3 dc in next dc; dc in next dc, ch 2; *dc in next dc, 3 dc in next dc; dc in next dc, ch 2; rep from * 6 times more; join in 3rd ch of beg ch-3—*40 dc*. Change to Color C by drawing lp through; cut Color B.

Rnd 4: Ch 3, 2 hdc in next dc; sc in next 3 dc, in next ch-2 sp, and in next 3 dc; 2 hdc in next dc; dc in next dc; *ch 3—*corner sp made*; dc in next dc, 2 hdc in next dc; sc in next 3 dc, in next ch-2 sp, and in next 3 dc; 2 hdc in next dc; dc in next dc; rep from * twice more; ch 3—*corner sp made*; join in 3rd ch of beg ch-3.

Rnd 5: Ch 1, sc in same sc and in next 12 sts; in next corner ch-3 sp work (2 hdc, dc, 2 hdc)—*hdc corner made*; *sc in next 13 sts, in next corner ch-3 sp work (2 hdc, dc, 2 hdc)—*hdc corner made*; rep from * twice more; join in first sc.

Finish off and weave in all ends. ●

Square 64

Materials
- Yarn—Color A off white; Color B dark turquoise

Pattern Stitch
Back Post Double Crochet (bpdc): Yo, insert hook from back to front to back around post *(see page 98)* of indicated st, draw up lp, [yo, draw through 2 lps on hook] twice—*bpdc made*.

Instructions
With Color A, ch 4; join to form a ring.

Rnd 1 (RS): Ch 3 *(counts as a dc on this and following rnds)*, 11 dc in ring; join in 3rd ch of beg ch-3—*12 dc*.

Rnd 2: Ch 3, **bpdc** *(see Pattern Stitch)* around beg ch-3 of Rnd 1; [dc in next dc, bpdc around same dc as last dc worked] 11 times; join in 3rd ch of beg ch-3—*24 dc*. Change to Color B by drawing lp through; cut Color A.

Rnd 3: Ch 1, 2 sc in same ch as joining; working in back lps only, sc in next 2 dc, [2 sc in next dc, sc in next 2 dc] 7 times; join in first sc—*32 sc*.

Rnd 4: Ch 4 *(counts as an hdc and a ch-2 sp)*, hdc in same sc—*beg corner made*; sc in next 7 sc; *in next sc work (hdc, ch 2, hdc)—*corner made*; sc in next 7 sc; rep from * twice more; join in 2nd ch of beg ch-4.

Rnd 5: Sl st in next ch-2 sp; change to Color A by drawing lp through; cut Color B; ch 3, in same sp work (3 tr, dc)—*beg tr corner made*; bpdc around each of next 9 sts; *in next corner ch-2 sp work (dc, 3 tr, dc)—*tr corner made*; bpdc around each of next 9 sts; rep from * twice more; join in 3rd ch of beg ch-3. Finish off Color A.

Rnd 6: Join Color B in back lp of 2nd tr of any corner; ch 5 *(counts as a dc and a ch-2 sp)*, dc in same sp—*beg dc corner made*; working in back lps only, hdc in next 13 sts; *in next tr work (dc, ch 2, dc)—*dc corner made*; hdc in next 13 sts; rep from * twice more; join in 3rd ch of beg ch-5.

Rnd 7: Ch 1, sc in same ch as joining; 3 sc in next corner ch-2 sp—*sc corner made*; *sc in next 15 sts, 3 sc in next corner ch-2 sp—*sc corner made*; rep from * twice more; sc in next 14 sts; join in first sc.

Finish off and weave in all ends. ●

Square 65

Materials
- Yarn—Color A light blue; Color B off white; Color C blue

Instructions
With Color A, ch 5; join to form a ring.

Rnd 1 (RS): Ch 3 *(counts as a dc)*, 15 dc in ring; join in 3rd ch of beg ch-3—*16 dc.*

Rnd 2: Ch 4 *(counts as a tr on this and following rnd)*, in same ch work (2 tr, ch 2, 3 tr)—*beg corner made*; sk next dc, 3 tr in next dc; sk next dc; *in next dc work (3 tr, ch 2, 3 tr)—*corner made*; sk next dc, 3 tr in next dc; sk next dc; rep from * twice more; join in 4th ch of beg ch-4. Finish off Color A.

Rnd 3: Join Color B in any corner ch-2 sp; beg corner in same sp; *[sk next 3 tr, 2 tr in sp between last skipped tr and next tr] twice; sk next 3 tr, in next corner ch-2 sp work corner; rep from * twice more; [sk next 3 tr, 2 tr in sp between last skipped tr and next tr] twice; sk next 3 tr; join in 4th ch of beg ch-4. Finish off Color B.

Note: Rnds 4–6 are worked in sps between sts.

Rnd 4: Join Color C in any corner ch-2 sp; ch 3, in same sp work (dc, ch 3, 2 dc)—*beg dc corner made*; [sk next tr, dc in next sp] 9 times; sk next tr; *in next corner ch-2 sp work (2 dc, ch 3, 2 dc)—*dc corner made*; [sk next tr, dc in next sp] 9 times; sk next tr; rep from * twice more; join in 3rd ch of beg ch-3. Finish off Color C.

Rnd 5: Join Color B in any corner ch-3 sp; beg dc corner in same sp; [sk next dc, dc in next sp] 12 times; *in next corner ch-3 sp work dc corner; [sk next dc, dc in next sp] 12 times; rep from * twice more; join in 3rd ch of beg ch-3. Finish off Color B.

Rnd 6: Join Color C in any corner ch-3 sp; beg dc corner in same sp; [sk next dc, dc in next sp] 15 times; * corner in next corner; [sk next dc, dc in next sp] 15 times; rep from * twice more; join in 3rd ch of beg ch-3.

Rnd 7: Ch 1, sc in same ch as joining and in next dc; 3 sc in next corner ch-3 sp—*sc corner made*; *sc in next dc, 3 sc in next corner ch-3 sp—*sc corner made*; rep from * twice more; sc in next 17 dc; join in first sc.

Finish off and weave in all ends. ●

Square 66

Materials
- Yarn—Color A off white; Color B blue

Pattern Stitch
Back Post Double Crochet (bpdc): Yo, insert hook from back to front to back around post (see page 98) of st indicated, draw up lp, [yo, draw through 2 lps on hook] twice—bpdc made.

Instructions
With Color A, ch 4; join to form a ring.

Rnd 1 (RS): Ch 3 (counts as a dc on this and following rnds), 11 dc in ring; join in 3rd ch of beg ch-3—12 dc.

Rnd 2: Ch 3, **bpdc** (see Pattern Stitch) around beg ch-3 of Rnd 1; 2 bpdc around each dc; join in 3rd ch of beg ch-3—24 sts. Change to Color B by drawing lp through; cut Color A.

Rnd 3: Ch 1, 2 sc in same ch as joining; working in back lps only, sc in next 2 dc, [2 sc in next dc, sc in next 2 dc] 7 times; join in back lp of first sc.

Rnd 4: Ch 4 (counts as an hdc and a ch-2 sp), hdc in same lp—beg corner made; working in back lps only, sc in next 7 sc; *in next sc work (hdc, ch 2, hdc)—corner made; sc in next 7 sc; rep from * twice more; join in 2nd ch of beg ch-4. Finish off Color B.

Rnd 5: Join Color A in any corner ch-2 sp; ch 3, in same sp work (3 tr, dc)—beg tr corner made; bpdc around each of next 9 sts; *in next corner ch-2 sp work (dc, 3 tr, dc)—tr corner made; bpdc around each of next 9 sts; rep from * twice more; join in 3rd ch of beg ch-3. Change to Color B by drawing lp through; cut Color A.

Rnd 6: Ch 2 (counts as an hdc), working in back lps only, hdc in next tr, in next tr work (sc, ch 3, sc)—sc corner made; *hdc in next 13 sts, in next tr work (sc, ch 3, sc)—sc corner made; rep from * twice more; hdc in next 11 sts; join in 2nd ch of beg ch-2.

Finish off and weave in all ends. ●

Square 67

Materials
- Yarn—Color A light gold; Color B light yellow; Color C dark blue

Pattern Stitches

Cluster (CL): Keeping last lp of each dc on hook, 2 dc in st indicated; yo and draw through all 3 lps on hook—*CL made.*

Double Triple Crochet (dtr): Yo 3 times, draw up lp in st indicated, [yo, draw through 2 lps on hook] 4 times—*dtr made.*

Instructions

With Color A, ch 6; join to form a ring.

Rnd 1 (RS): Ch 2, dc in ring—beg CL made; ch 3, [**CL** *(see Pattern Stitches)* in ring, ch 3] 7 times; join in top of beg CL—*8 CLs and 8 ch-3 sps.* Finish off Color A.

Rnd 2: Join Color B in any ch-3 sp; ch 3 *(counts as a dc on this and following rnds)*, 4 dc in same sp; 5 dc in each rem ch-3 sp; join in 3rd ch of beg ch-3—*40 dc.* Change to Color C by drawing lp through; cut Color B.

Rnd 3: Ch 1, sc in same ch as joining; ch 3, sk next dc, sc in next dc; *ch 6, sc in 2nd ch from hook, hdc in next ch, dc in next ch, tr in next ch, **dtr** *(see Pattern Stitches)* in next ch—petal made; sk next 2 dc, sc in next dc,ch 3, sk next dc, sc in next dc; rep from * 6 times more; ch 6, sc in 2nd ch from hook, hdc in next ch, dc in next ch, tr in next ch, dtr in next ch—petal made; join in first sc—8 petals. Finish off Color C.

Rnd 4: Join Color A in any ch-3 sp; ch 4 *(counts as a tr)*, 2 tr in same sp; ch 3, sc in unused ch at tip of next petal, ch 3; *3 tr in next ch-3 sp; ch 3, sc in unused ch at tip of next petal, ch 3; rep from * 6 times more; join in 4th ch of beg ch-4. Finish off Color A.

Rnd 5: Join Color B in any sc; ch 3, in same sc work (2 dc, ch 3, 3 dc)—*beg corner made;* sc in next ch-3 sp, ch 5, 2 sc in next ch-3 sp; sc in next sc, 2 sc in next ch-3 sp; ch 5, sc in next ch-3 sp; *in next sc work (3 dc, ch 3, 3 dc)—corner made;* sc in next ch-3 sp, ch 5, 2 sc in next ch-3 sp; sc in next sc, 2 sc in next ch-3 sp; ch 5, sc in next ch-3 sp; rep from * twice more; join in 3rd ch of beg ch-3.

Rnd 6: Ch 3, hdc in next 2 dc, 5 sc in next corner ch-3 sp—*sc corner made;* hdc in next 2 dc, dc in next 2 sts, in next ch-5 sp work (dc, hdc, 3 sc); sc in next 5 sc, in next ch-5 sp work (3 sc, hdc, dc); *dc in next 2 sts, hdc in next 2 dc, 5 sc in next corner ch-3 sp—*sc corner made;* hdc in next 2 dc, dc in next 2 sts, in next ch-5 sp work (dc, hdc, 3 sc); sc in next 5 sc, in next ch-5 sp work (3 sc, hdc, dc); rep from * twice more; dc in next st; join in 3rd ch of beg ch-3.

Rnd 7: Ch 1, sc in same ch as joining and in next 4 sts; 3 sc in next sc—*3-sc corner made;* *sc in next 27 sts, 3 sc in next sc—*3-sc corner made;* rep from * twice more; sc in next 22 sts; join in first sc.

Finish off and weave in all ends. ●

Square 68

Materials
- Yarn—Color A light gold; Color B purple; Color C yellow

Pattern Stitches

Cluster (CL): Keeping last lp of each dc on hook, 3 dc in sp indicated; yo and draw through all 4 lps on hook—*CL made.*

Berry Stitch (berry st): Draw up lp in st indicated, ch 3, yo and draw through 2 lps on hook—*berry st made.*

Instructions

Flower

Make 3

With Color A and leaving a 12" end for sewing, ch 2.

Rnd 1 (RS): 5 sc in 2nd ch from hook; join in first sc. Change to Color B by drawing lp through; cut Color A.

Rnd 2: Ch 3, in same sc work (**CL**—*see Pattern Stitches*, ch 3, sl st)—*beg petal made*; in each rem sc work (sl st, ch 3, CL, ch 3, sl st)—*petal made*; join in joining sl st—*5 petals.*

Finish off.

Square

With Color C, ch 6; join to form a ring.

Rnd 1 (RS): Ch 3 *(counts as a dc on this and following rnds)*, 11 dc in ring; join in 3rd ch of beg ch-3—*12 dc.*

Rnd 2: Ch 3, dc in same ch as joining; ch 1, [2 dc in next dc, ch 1] 11 times; join in 3rd ch of beg ch-3—*24 dc.*

Rnd 3: Ch 3, dc in next dc, ch 2, sk next ch-1 sp, dc in next 2 dc, ch 2, sk next ch-1 sp, CL in next dc; ch 5— *corner lp made*; CL in next dc; *[ch 2, sk next ch-1 sp, dc in next 2 dc] twice; ch 2, sk next ch-1 sp, CL in next dc; ch 5—*corner lp made*; CL in next dc; rep from * twice more; ch 2; join in 3rd ch of beg ch-3.

Rnd 4: Ch 3, dc in next dc, ch 2, dc in next 2 dc, ch 2, in next corner lp work (CL, ch 1, CL, ch 1, CL)—*CL corner made*; *[ch 2, dc in next 2 dc] twice; ch 2, in next corner lp work (CL, ch 1, CL, ch 1, CL)—*CL corner made*; rep from * twice more; ch 2; join in 3rd ch of beg ch-3.

Rnd 5: Ch 3, dc in next dc, ch 2, dc in next 2 dc, 2 dc in next ch-2 sp; dc in next CL, 2 dc in next ch-1 sp; in next CL work (CL, ch 2, CL)—*ch-2 corner made*; 2 dc in next ch-1 sp; dc in next CL, 2 dc in next ch-2 sp; *dc in next 2 dc, ch 2, dc in next 2 dc, 2 dc in next ch-2 sp; dc in next CL, 2 dc in next ch-1 sp; in next CL work (CL, ch 2, CL)—*ch-2 corner made*; 2 dc in next ch-1 sp; dc in next CL, 2 dc in next ch-2 sp; rep from * twice more; join in 3rd ch of beg ch-3. Finish off Color C.

Rnd 6: Join Color A in any corner ch-2 sp; ch 1, 3 sc in same sp—*sc corner made*; **berry st** *(see Pattern Stitches)* in next CL; [sc in next dc, berry st in next dc] 3 times; sc in next dc, 2 sc in next ch-2 sp; sc in next dc, [berry st in next dc, sc in next dc] 3 times; berry st in next CL; *3 sc in next corner ch-2 sp—*sc corner made*; berry st in next CL; [sc in next dc, berry st in next dc] 3 times; sc in next dc, 2 sc in next ch-2 sp; sc in next dc, [berry st in next dc, sc in next dc] 3 times; berry st in next CL; rep from * twice more; join in first sc. Finish off Color A.

Rnd 7: Join Color B in 2nd sc of any sc corner; ch 1, sc corner in same sc; sc in next 20 sts; *sc corner in next sc; sc in next 20 sts; rep from * twice more; join in first sc.

Finish off.

Finishing

Referring to photo for placement and with tapestry needle, tack Flowers to center of Square. Weave in all ends. ●

Square 69

Materials
• Yarn—Color light purple

Pattern Stitches
Beginning Cluster (beg CL): Ch 2, keeping last lp of each dc on hook, 2 dc in st indicated; yo and draw through all 3 lps on hook—*beg CL made*.

Cluster (CL): Keeping last lp of each dc on hook, 3 dc in st indicated; yo and draw through all 4 lps on hook—*CL made*.

Instructions
Ch 6, join to form a ring.

Rnd 1 (RS): Ch 3 *(counts as a dc on this and following rnds)*, 11 dc in ring; join in 3rd ch of beg ch-3—*12 dc*.

Rnd 2: Beg CL *(see Pattern Stitches)* in same ch; [ch 1, **CL** *(see Pattern Stitches)* in next dc] twice; ch 5; *[CL in next dc, ch 1] twice; CL in next dc; ch 5; rep from * twice more; join in top of beg CL.

Rnd 3: Sl st in next ch-1 sp, beg CL in same sp; ch 1, CL in next ch-1 sp; ch 1, in next ch-5 sp work (3 dc, ch 2, 3 dc)—*corner made*; ch 1; *[CL in next ch-1 sp, ch 1] twice; in next ch-5 sp work (3 dc, ch 2, 3 dc)—*corner made*; ch 1; rep from * twice more; join in top of beg CL.

Rnd 4: Sl st in next ch-1 sp, beg CL in same sp; ch 2, sk next ch-1 sp, dc in next 3 dc; *in next corner ch-2 sp work (dc, ch 1, tr, ch 1, dc)—*tr corner made*; dc in next 3 dc, ch 2, sk next ch-1 sp, CL in next ch-1 sp; ch 2, sk next ch-1 sp, dc in next 3 dc; rep from * twice more; in next corner ch-2 sp work (dc, ch 1, tr, ch 1, dc)—*tr corner made*; dc in next 3 dc, ch 2, sk next ch-1 sp; join in top of beg CL.

Rnd 5: Sl st in next ch-2 sp, ch 1, 2 sc in same sp; sc in next 4 dc and in next ch-1 sp; *3 sc in next tr—*sc corner made*; sc in next ch-1 sp and in next 4 dc, 2 sc in each of next 2 ch-2 sps; sc in next 4 dc and in next ch-1 sp; rep from * twice more; 3 sc in next tr—*sc corner made*; sc in next ch-1 sp and in next 4 dc, 2 sc in next ch-2 sp; join in first sc.

Finish off and weave in ends. ●

Square 70

Materials

- Yarn—Color A red; Color B light turquoise; Color C dark turquoise

Instructions

With Color A, ch 8; join to form a ring.

Rnd 1 (RS): Ch 3 *(counts as a dc on this and following rnds)*, 15 dc in ring; join in 3rd ch of beg ch-3—*16 dc.*

Rnd 2: Sl st between ch-3 and next dc; ch 5 *(counts as a dc and ch-2 sp)*, [dc between next 2 dc, ch 2] 15 times; join in 3rd ch of beg ch-5.

Rnd 3: Sl st in next ch-2 sp, ch 3, 2 dc in same sp; ch 1, [3 dc in next ch-2 sp, ch 1] 15 times; join in 3rd ch of beg ch-3—*48 dc.* Finish off Color A.

Rnd 4: Join Color B in any ch-1 sp; ch 1, sc in same sp; *ch 5, sc in next ch-1 sp, [ch 3, sc in next ch-1 sp] 3 times; rep from * twice more; ch 5, sc in next ch-1 sp, [ch 3, sc in next ch-1 sp] twice; ch 3; join in first sc.

Rnd 5: Sl st in next ch-5 sp, ch 3, in same sp work (2 dc, ch 2, 3 dc)—*beg corner made*; 3 dc in each of next 3 ch-3 sps; *in next ch-5 sp work (3 dc, ch 2, 3 dc)—*corner made*; 3 dc in each of next 3 ch-3 sps; rep from * twice more; join in 3rd ch of beg ch-3. Finish off Color B.

Rnd 6: Join Color C in any corner ch-2 sp; ch 3, in same sp work (tr, dc)—*beg tr corner made*; [dc between next 2 dc] 14 times; *in next corner ch-2 sp work (dc, tr, dc)—*tr corner made*; [dc between next 2 dc] 14 times; rep from * twice more; join in 3rd ch of beg ch-3.

Finish off and weave in all ends. ●

Square 71

Materials

- Yarn—Color A pink; Color B emerald green

Instructions

With Color A, ch 5; join to form a ring.

Rnd 1 (RS): Ch 6 *(counts as a dc and a ch-3 sp)*, [dc in ring, ch 3] 7 times; join in 3rd ch of beg ch-6—*8 ch-3 sps.*

Rnd 2: Sl st in next ch-3 sp, ch 3 *(counts as a dc on this and following rnds)*, in same sp work (2 dc, ch 2, 3 dc)—*beg corner made*; ch 1, sc in next ch-3 sp, ch 1; *in next ch-3 sp work (3 dc, ch 2, 3 dc)—*corner made*; ch 1, sc in next ch-3 sp, ch 1; rep from * twice more; join in 3rd ch of beg ch-3. Finish off Color A.

Rnd 3: Join Color B in any corner ch-2 sp; beg corner in same sp; ch 2, tr in next sc, ch 2; *in next corner ch-2 sp work corner; ch 2, tr in next sc, ch 2; rep from * twice more; join in 3rd ch of beg ch-3.

Rnd 4: Ch 1, sc in same ch and in next 2 dc; 3 sc in next corner ch-2 sp—*sc corner made*; *sc in next 3 dc, 2 sc in next ch-2 sp; sc in next tr, 2 sc in next ch-2 sp; sc in next 3 dc, 3 sc in next corner ch-2 sp—*sc corner made*; rep from * twice more; sc in next 3 dc, 2 sc in next ch-2 sp; sc in next tr, 2 sc in next ch-2 sp; join in first sc.

Finish off and weave in all ends. ●

Square 72

Materials
- Yarn—Color A off white; Color B lavender; Color C purple

Pattern Stitch
Long Double Crochet (long dc): Yo, insert hook in next ch-1 sp on 2nd rnd below, draw up lp to height of working rnd, [yo, draw through 2 lps on hook] twice—*long dc made*.

Instructions
With Color A, ch 8; join to form a ring.

Rnd 1 (RS): Ch 3 *(counts as a dc on this and following rnds)*, dc in ring, ch 2, [2 dc in ring, ch 2] 7 times; join in 3rd ch of beg ch-3—*8 ch-2 sps*. Finish off Color A.

Rnd 2: Join Color B in any ch-2 sp; ch 3, in same sp work (dc, ch 2, 2 dc)—*beg shell made*; ch 1; *in next ch-2 sp work (2 dc, ch 2, 2 dc)—*shell made*; ch 1; rep from * 6 times more; join in 3rd ch of beg ch-3—*8 shells*. Change to Color C by drawing lp through; cut Color B.

Rnd 3: Ch 3, dc in next dc, in next ch-2 sp work (dc, ch 2, dc)—*V-st made*; *dc in next 2 dc, ch 1, in ch-2 sp of next shell work shell; ch 1, sk next ch-1 sp, dc in next 2 dc, in next ch-2 sp work (dc, ch 2, dc)—*V-st made*; rep from * twice more; dc in next 2 dc, ch 1, in ch-2 sp of next shell work shell; ch 1, sk next ch-1 sp; join in 3rd ch of beg ch-3. Finish off Color C.

Rnd 4: Join Color A in ch-2 sp of any V-st; beg shell in same sp; dc in next 3 dc, **long dc** *(see Pattern Stitch)* in next ch-1 sp on 2nd rnd below; shell in next shell; long dc in next ch-1 sp on 2nd rnd below; dc in next 3 dc; *shell in ch-2 sp of next V-st; dc in next 3 dc, long dc in next ch-1 sp on 2nd rnd below; shell in next shell; long dc in next ch-1 sp on 2nd rnd below; dc in next 3 dc; rep from * twice more; join in 3rd ch of beg ch-3.

Rnd 5: Sl st in next dc and in next ch-2 sp, ch 1, in same sp work (sc, ch 3, sc)—*corner made*; ch 4, sk next 3 dc, sc in next dc, ch 4, sk next 4 sts, sc in next ch-2 sp, ch 4, sk next 4 sts, sc in next dc, ch 4, sk next 3 dc; * in next ch-2 sp work (sc, ch 3, sc)—*corner made*; ch 4, sk next 3 dc, sc in next dc, ch 4, sk next 4 sts, sc in next ch-2 sp, ch 4, sk next 4 sts, sc in next dc, ch 4, sk next 3 dc; rep from * twice more; join in first sc.

Rnd 6: Sl st in next corner ch-3 sp, ch 3, in same sp work (2 dc, ch 2, 3 dc)—*beg dc corner made*; 4 dc in next ch-4 sp; in next ch-4 sp work (2 hdc, sc); sc in next sc, in next ch-4 sp work (sc, 2 hdc); 4 dc in next ch-4 sp; *in next corner ch-3 sp work (3 dc, ch 2, 3 dc)—*dc corner made*; 4 dc in next ch-4 sp; in next ch-4 sp work (2 hdc, sc); sc in next sc, in next ch-4 sp work (sc, 2 hdc); 4 dc in next ch-4 sp; rep from * twice more; join in 3rd ch of beg ch-3.

Rnd 7: Ch 1, sc in same ch as joining and in next 2 dc; 3 sc in next corner ch-2 sp—*sc corner made*; *sc in next 21 sts, 3 sc in next corner ch-2 sp—*sc corner made*; rep from * twice more; sc in next 18 sts; join in first sc.

Finish off and weave in all ends. ●

Square 73

Materials
- Yarn—Color A gold; Color B off white; Color C emerald green

Instructions

Flower

Center
With Color A, ch 5; join to form a ring.

Rnd 1 (RS): Ch 1, 8 sc in ring; join in front lp of first sc.

Rnd 2: Ch 1, in same sp work (sc, ch 3, sc, ch 3, sc); in front lp of each rem sc work (sc, ch 3, sc, ch 3, sc); join in first sc. Finish off Color A.

Rnd 3: Working behind prev rnd, join Color B in unused lp of any sc of Rnd 1; ch 1, 2 sc in same lp and in each rem unused lp; join in back lp of first sc—*16 sc*.

Rnd 4: Ch 1, sc in same lp; working in back lps only, sc in each rem sc; join in first sc.

Rnd 5: Ch 1, 2 sc in same sc and in each rem sc; join in front lp of first sc—*32 sc*.

First Petal
Row 1 (RS): Ch 1, sc in same lp and in front lps of next 2 sc. Ch 1, turn.

Row 2: 2 sc in next sc; sc in next sc, 2 sc in next sc—*5 sc*. Ch 1, turn.

Row 3: 2 sc in next sc; sc in next 3 sc, 2 sc in next sc—*7 sc*. Ch 1, turn.

Row 4: 2 sc in next sc; sc in next 5 sc, 2 sc in next sc—*9 sc*. Ch 1, turn.

Row 5: Sc in each sc. Ch 1, turn.

Row 6: Dec over next 2 sc *(to work dec: draw up lp in each of next 2 sc, yo and draw through all 3 lps on hook—dec made)*; sc in next 5 sc, dec as before over next 2 sc—*7 sc*. Ch 1, turn.

Row 7: Dec; sc in next 3 sc, dec—*5 sc*. Ch 1, turn.

Row 8: Dec; sc in next sc, dec—*3 sc*. Ch 1, turn.

Row 9: 3-sc dec over next 3 sc *(to work 3-sc dec: draw up lp in each of next 3 sc, yo and draw through all 4 lps on hook—3-sc dec made)*. Finish off, leaving an 8" end for sewing.

2nd–8th Petals

Join Color B in front lp of 2nd sc on Rnd 5 from last petal made. Work same as for first petal.

Square

Hold piece with right side facing you; working behind petals, join Color C in unused lp of any sc on Rnd 5 of Flower Center.

Rnd 1 (RS): Ch 1, sc in same lp and in unused lp of each rem sc; join in first sc—*32 sc*.

Rnd 2: Ch 3 *(counts as a dc on this and following rnds)*, in same sc work (dc, ch 2, 2 dc)—*beg corner made*; hdc in next 2 sc, sc in next 3 sc, hdc in next 2 sc; *in next sc work (2 dc, ch 2, 2 dc)—*corner made*; hdc in next 2 sc, sc in next 3 sc, hdc in next 2 sc; rep from * twice more; join in 3rd ch of beg ch-3.

Rnd 3: Ch 3, dc in next dc, in next corner ch-2 sp work corner; *dc in next 11 sts, in next corner ch-2 sp work corner; rep from * twice more; dc in next 9 sts; join in 3rd ch of beg ch-3.

Rnd 4: Ch 3, dc in next 3 dc, corner in next corner; *dc in next 15 dc, corner in next corner; rep from * twice more; dc in next 11 dc; join in 3rd ch of beg ch-3.

Rnd 5: Ch 3, dc in next 5 dc, corner in next corner; *dc in next 19 dc, corner in next corner; rep from * twice more; dc in next 13 dc; join in 3rd ch of beg ch-3.

Rnd 6: Ch 1, sc in same ch as joining and in next 7 dc; 3 sc in next corner ch-2 sp—*sc corner made*; *sc in next 23 dc, 3 sc in next corner ch-2 sp—*sc corner made*; rep from * twice more; sc in next 15 dc; join in first sc. Finish off.

Finishing

Referring to photo for placement and with tapestry needle, tack petals to Square. Weave in all ends. ●

Square 74

Materials

- Yarn—Color A light gold; Color B blue; Color C off white

Pattern Stitch

Popcorn (PC): 5 dc in ring or sp indicated; drop lp from hook, insert hook in first dc made, draw dropped lp through—*PC made*.

Instructions

With Color A, ch 6; join to form a ring.

Rnd 1 (RS): Ch 1, sc in ring, ch 3, **PC** *(see Pattern Stitch)* in ring; ch 3; *sc in ring, ch 3, PC in ring; ch 3; rep from * twice more; join in first sc—*4 PCs*.

Rnd 2: Ch 1, sc in same sc; ch 7, [sc in next sc, ch 7] 3 times; join in first sc—*4 ch-7 sps*.

Rnd 3: Ch 1, sc in same sc; ch 5, PC in next ch-7 sp; ch 5; *sc in next sc, ch 5, PC in next ch-7 sp; ch 5; rep from * twice more; join in first sc. Finish off Color A.

Rnd 4: Join Color B in top of any PC; ch 3 *(counts as a dc on this and following rnds)*, in same sp work (2 dc, ch 2, 3 dc)—*beg corner made*; ch 1, [3 dc in next ch-5 sp, ch 1] twice; *in top of next PC work (3 dc, ch 2, 3 dc)—*corner made*; ch 1, [3 dc in next ch-5 sp, ch 1] twice; rep from * twice more; join in 3rd ch of beg ch-3. Finish off Color B.

Rnd 5: Join Color C in any corner ch-2 sp; beg corner in same sp; ch 1, [3 dc in next ch-1 sp, ch 1] 3 times; *in next corner ch-2 sp work corner; ch 1, [3 dc in next ch-1 sp, ch 1] 3 times; rep from * twice more; join in 3rd ch of beg ch-3.

Rnd 6: Ch 1, sc in same ch and in next 2 dc, 3 sc in next corner ch-2 sp—*sc corner made*; working in each dc and in each ch-1 sp, *sc in next 19 sts, 3 sc in next corner ch-2 sp—*sc corner made*; rep from * twice more; sc in next 16 sts; join in first sc.

Finish off and weave in all ends. ●

Square 75

Materials
• Yarn—Color A off white; Color B blue

Pattern Stitch

Long Triple Crochet (long tr): Yo twice, insert hook in next ch-1 sp on 2nd rnd below, draw up lp to height of working rnd, [yo, draw through 2 lps on hook 3 times—*long tr made*.

Instructions

With Color A, ch 4; join to form a ring.

Rnd 1 (RS): Ch 4 *(counts as a dc and a ch-1 sp)*, [dc in ring, ch 1] 7 times; join in 3rd ch of beg ch-4—*8 dc*.

Rnd 2: Ch 3 *(counts as a dc on this and following rnds)*, 2 dc in same ch as joining; 3 dc in each rem dc; join in 3rd ch of beg ch-3—*24 dc*. Change to Color B by drawing lp through; cut Color A.

Rnd 3: Ch 1, sc in same ch as joining; ch 1, sk next dc, sc in next dc, **long tr** *(see Pattern Stitch)* in next ch-1 sp on 2nd rnd below, sc in next dc, ch 1, sk next dc; *sc in next dc, long tr in next ch-1 sp on 2nd rnd below, sc in next dc, ch 1, sk next dc; rep from * 6 times more; join in first sc.

Rnd 4: Sl st in next ch-1 sp, ch 1, sc in same sp; ch 1, sk next sc, in next long tr work (dc, ch 1, tr, ch 1, dc)—*corner made*; ch 1, sk next sc, sc in next ch-1 sp, ch 1, sk next sc, sc in next long tr, ch 1, sk next sc; *sc in next ch-1 sp, ch 1, sk next sc, in next long tr work (dc, ch 1, tr, ch 1, dc)—*corner made*; ch 1, sk next sc, sc in next ch-1 sp, ch 1, sk next sc, sc in next long tr, ch 1, sk next sc; rep from * twice more; join in first sc.

Rnd 5: Ch 1, sc in same sc; ch 1, sk next ch-1 sp, sc in next st, ch 1, in next tr work (sc, ch 3, sc)—*sc corner made*; *[ch 1, sk next ch-1 sp, sc in next st] 5 times; ch 1, in next tr work (sc, ch 3, sc)—*sc corner made*; rep from * twice more; [ch 1, sk next ch-1 sp, sc in next st] 3 times; ch 1; join in first sc. Finish off Color B.

Rnd 6: Join Color A in first sc of any corner; ch 1, sc in same sc; ch 3—*corner sp made*; *sc in next sc, [ch 1, sc in next sc] 6 times; ch 3—*corner sp made*; rep from * twice more; sc in next sc, [ch 1, sc in next sc] 5 times; ch 1; join in first sc.

Finish off and weave in all ends. ●

Square 76

Materials
- Yarn—Color A yellow; Color B blue; Color C off white

Instructions
With Color A, ch 6; join to form a ring.

Rnd 1 (RS): Ch 1, 12 sc in ring; join in first sc.

Rnd 2: Ch 3 *(counts as a dc on this and following rnds)*, dc in same sc; 2 dc in each rem sc; join in 3rd ch of beg ch-3—*24 dc*. Finish off Color A.

Rnd 3: Join Color B between any 2 dc; ch 1, sc in same sp; ch 3, sk next 3 dc; *sc in sp between last dc skipped and next dc, ch 3, sk next 3 dc; rep from * 6 times more; join in first sc—*8 sc*.

Rnd 4: Ch 1, sc in same sc; in next ch-3 sp work (hdc, dc, 3 tr, dc, hdc); *sc in next sc, in next ch-3 sp work (hdc, dc, 3 tr, dc, hdc); rep from * 6 times more; join in first sc. Finish off Color B.

Rnd 5: Join Color C in 2nd tr of any 3-tr group; ch 6 *(counts as a dc and a ch-3 sp)*, dc in same tr—*beg corner made*; ch 6, sc in 2nd tr of next 3-tr group, ch 6; *in 2nd tr of next 3-tr group work (dc, ch 3, dc)—*corner made*; ch 6, sc in 2nd tr of next 3-tr group, ch 6; rep from * twice more; join in 3rd ch of beg ch-3.

Rnd 6: Sl st in next corner ch-3 sp, ch 3, in same sp work (2 dc, ch 1, 3 dc)—*beg dc corner made*; 6 dc in each of next 2 ch-6 sps; *in next corner ch-3 sp work (3 dc, ch 1, 3 dc)—*dc corner made*; 6 dc in each of next 2 ch-6 sps; rep from * twice more; join in 3rd ch of beg ch-3.

Rnd 7: Ch 3, dc in next 2 dc, 3 dc in next corner ch-1 sp—*3-dc corner made*; *dc in next 18 dc, 3 dc in next corner ch-1 sp—*3-dc corner made*; rep from * twice more; dc in next 15 dc; join in 3rd ch of beg ch-3.

Finish off and weave in all ends. ●

Square 77

Materials
- Yarn—Color pink

Pattern Stitch

Double Triple Crochet (dtr): Yo 3 times, draw up lp in st indicated, [yo, draw through 2 lps on hook] 4 times—*dtr made.*

Instructions

Ch 10.

Rnd 1 (RS): Sl st in 8th ch from hook, [ch 9, sl st in 8th ch from hook] 7 times; join in first ch of beg ch-10—*8 ch-7 sps.*

Rnd 2: Sl st in next unused ch of beg ch-10; ch 10 *(counts as a dtr and a ch-5 sp)*, sc in next ch-7 sp, ch 5; *****dtr** *(see Pattern Stitch)* in next unused ch of beg ch-10, ch 5, sc in next ch-7 sp, ch 5; rep from * 6 times more; join in 5th ch of beg ch-10—*16 ch-5 sps.*

Rnd 3: Sl st in next ch-5 sp, ch 1, sc in same sp; ch 5, [sc in next ch-5 sp, ch 5] 15 times; join in first sc.

Rnd 4: Sl st in next ch-5 sp, ch 4 *(counts as a tr)*, in same sp work (2 tr, ch 3, 3 tr)—*beg corner made*; ch 1, 3 dc in next ch-5 sp; ch 1, 3 hdc in next ch-5 sp; ch 1, 3 dc in next ch-5 sp; ch 1; *in next ch-5 sp work (3 tr, ch 3, 3 tr)—*corner made*; ch 1, 3 dc in next ch-5 sp; ch 1, 3 hdc in next ch-5 sp; ch 1, 3 dc in next ch-5 sp; ch 1; rep from * twice more; join in 4th ch of beg ch-4.

Rnd 5: Ch 1, sc in same ch as joining and in next 2 tr; 3 sc in next corner ch-3 sp—*sc corner made*; working in each st and in each ch, *sc in next 19 sts, 3 sc in next corner ch-3 sp—*sc corner made*; rep from * twice more; sc in next 16 sts; join in first sc.

Finish off and weave in ends. ●

Square 78

Materials

• Yarn—Color blue

Instructions

Ch 6, join to form a ring.

Rnd 1 (RS): Ch 3 *(counts as a dc)*, 3 dc in ring; ch 3, [4 dc in ring, ch 3] 3 times; join in 3rd ch of beg ch-3—*16 dc.*

Note: Rnds 2 through 5 are worked in back lps only.

Rnd 2: Ch 5 *(counts as a dc and a ch-2 sp on this and following rnds)*, sk next 2 dc, dc in next dc and in next ch; *in next ch work (dc, ch 3, dc)—*corner made*; dc in next ch and in next dc, ch 2, sk next 2 dc, dc in next dc and in next ch; rep from * twice more; in next ch work (dc, ch 3, dc)—*corner made*; dc in next ch; join in 3rd ch of beg ch-5.

Rnd 3: Ch 5, sk next ch-2 sp, dc in next 3 dc and in next ch, in next ch work corner; *dc in next ch and in next 3 dc, ch 2, sk next ch-2 sp, dc in next 3 dc and in next ch, in next ch work corner; rep from * twice more; dc in next ch and in next 2 dc; join in 3rd ch of beg ch-5.

Rnd 4: Ch 5, sk next ch-2 sp, dc in next 5 dc and in next ch, corner in next ch; *dc in next ch and in next 5 dc, ch 2, sk next ch-2 sp, dc in next 5 dc and in next ch, corner in next ch; rep from * twice more; dc in next ch and in next 4 dc; join in 3rd ch of beg ch-5.

Rnd 5: Ch 5; sk next ch-2 sp, dc in next 7 dc and in next ch, corner in next ch; *dc in next ch and in next 7 dc, ch 2, sk next ch-2 sp, dc in next 7 dc and in next ch, corner in next ch; rep from * twice more; dc in next ch and in next 6 dc; join in 3rd ch of beg ch-5.

Note: Following rnd is worked through both lps.

Rnd 6: Ch 1, sc in same ch as joining; 2 sc in next ch-2 sp; sc in next 9 dc, 3 sc in next corner ch-3 sp—*sc corner made*; *sc in next 9 dc, 2 sc in next ch-2 sp; sc in next 9 sc, 3 sc in next corner ch-3 sp—*sc corner made*; rep from * twice more; sc in next 8 dc; join in first sc.

Finish off and weave in ends. ●

Square 79

Materials
- Yarn—Color A lavender; Color B purple; Color C yellow

Pattern Stitches
Beginning Popcorn (beg PC): Ch 3, 3 dc in sp indicated; drop lp from hook, insert hook in 3rd ch of beg ch-3, draw dropped lp through—*beg PC made*.

Popcorn (PC): 4 dc in sp indicated; drop lp from hook, insert hook in first dc; draw dropped lp through—*PC made*.

Instructions
With Color A, ch 4; join to form a ring.

Rnd 1 (RS): Ch 4 *(counts as a dc and a ch-1 sp on this and following rnds)*, [dc in ring, ch 1] 11 times; join in 3rd ch of beg ch-4—*12 ch-1 sps*.

Rnd 2: Sl st in next ch-1 sp, **beg PC** *(see Pattern Stitches)* in same sp; ch 3; [**PC** *(see Pattern Stitches)* in next ch-1 sp, ch 3] 11 times; join in top of beg PC. Finish off Color A.

Rnd 3: Join Color B in any ch-3 sp; in same sp work (beg PC, ch 3, PC)—*beg corner made*; [ch 3, PC in next ch-3 sp] twice; ch 3; *in next ch-3 sp work (PC, ch 3, PC)—*corner made*; [ch 3, PC in next ch-3 sp] twice; ch 3; rep from * twice more; join in top of beg PC. Finish off Color B.

Rnd 4: Join Color C in any corner ch-3 sp; ch 6 *(counts as a dc and a ch-3 sp)*, dc in same sp—*beg dc corner made*; [ch 3, sc in next ch-3 sp] 3 times; ch 3; *in next ch-3 sp work (dc, ch 3, dc)—*dc corner made*; [ch 3, sc in next ch-3 sp] 3 times; ch 3; rep from * twice more; join in 3rd ch of beg ch-6. Finish off Color C.

Rnd 5: Join Color B in any corner ch-3 sp; ch 1, 3 sc in same sp—*sc corner made*; sc in next dc, [3 sc in next ch-3 sp, sc in next sc] 3 times; 3 sc in next ch-3 sp; sc in next dc; *3 sc in next corner ch-3 sp—*sc corner made*; sc in next dc, [3 sc in next ch-3 sp, sc in next sc] 3 times; 3 sc in next ch-3 sp; sc in next dc; rep from * twice more; join in first sc.

Finish off and weave in all ends. ●

Square 80

Materials
- Yarn—Color light blue

Pattern Stitches
Beginning Popcorn (beg PC): Ch 3, 4 dc in st indicated; drop lp from hook, insert hook in 3rd ch of beg ch-3, draw dropped lp through—*beg PC made*.

Popcorn (PC): 5 dc in st indicated; drop lp from hook, insert hook in first dc made, draw dropped lp through—*PC made*.

Instructions
Ch 8, join to form a ring.

Rnd 1 (RS): Ch 1, 8 sc in ring; join in first sc.

Rnd 2: Ch 1, sc in same sc; ch 15, sk next sc, [sc in next sc, ch 15, sk next sc] 3 times; join in first sc—*4 ch-15 sps*.

Rnd 3: Beg PC *(see Pattern Stitches)* in same sc; in next ch-15 sp work (sc, hdc, 5 dc, ch 5, sc, ch 5, 5 dc, hdc, sc); ***PC** (see Pattern Stitches)* in next sc; in next ch-15 sp work (sc, hdc, 5 dc, ch 5, sc, ch 5, 5 dc, hdc, sc); rep from * twice more; join in top of beg PC—*4 PCs*.

Rnd 4: Ch 7 *(counts as a tr and a ch-3 sp)*, sk next 4 sts, sc in next dc, ch 3, sc in next ch-5 sp, ch 5—*corner sp made*; sc in next ch-5 sp, ch 3, sk next 2 sts, sc in next dc, ch 3, sk next 4 sts; *tr in top of next PC, ch 3, sk next 4 sts, sc in next dc, ch 3, sc in next ch-5 sp, ch 5—*corner sp made*; sc in next ch-5 sp, ch 3, sk next 2 sts, sc in next dc, ch 3, sk next 4 sts; rep from * twice more; join in 4th ch of beg ch-7.

Rnd 5: Sl st in next ch-3 sp, ch 3 *(counts as a dc)*, 2 dc in same sp; 3 dc in next ch-3 sp; in next ch-5 sp work (3 dc, ch 2, 3 dc)—*corner made*; *3 dc in each of next 4 ch-3 sps; in next ch-5 sp work (3 dc, ch 2, 3 dc)—*corner made*; rep from * twice more; 3 dc in each of next 2 ch-3 sps; join in 3rd ch of beg ch-3.

Rnd 6: Ch 1, sc in same ch as joining and in next 8 dc; 3 sc in next corner ch-2 sp—*sc corner made*; *sc in next 18 dc, 3 sc in next corner ch-2 sp—*sc corner made*; rep from * twice more; sc in next 9 dc; join in first sc.

Finish off and weave in ends. ●

Square 81

Materials
- Yarn—Color A yellow; Color B light turquoise; Color C red; Color D dark turquoise

Instructions
With Color A, ch 6; join to form a ring.

Rnd 1 (RS): Ch 1; *3 sc in ring; ch 10—*corner lp made*; rep from * 3 times more; join in first sc. Change to Color B by drawing lp through; cut Color A.

Rnd 2: Ch 2 *(counts as an hdc on this and following rnds)*, hdc in same sc and in next sc; 2 hdc in next sc; ch 12—*corner lp made*; *2 hdc in next sc; hdc in next sc, 2 hdc in next sc; ch 12—*corner lp made*; rep from * twice more; join in 2nd ch of beg ch-2. Change to Color C by drawing lp through; cut Color B.

Rnd 3: Ch 3 *(counts as a dc on this and following rnds)*, dc in same ch as joining and in next 3 hdc; 2 dc in next hdc; ch 12—*corner lp made*; *2 dc in next hdc; dc in next 3 hdc, 2 dc in next hdc; ch 12—*corner lp made*; rep from * twice more; join in 3rd ch of beg ch-3. Change to Color D by drawing lp through; cut Color C.

Rnd 4: Ch 3, dc in same ch as joining and in next 5 dc; 2 dc in next dc; ch 12—*corner lp made*; *2 dc in next dc; dc in next 5 dc, 2 dc in next dc; ch 12—*corner lp made*; rep from * twice more; join in 3rd ch of beg ch-3. Change to Color A by drawing lp through; cut Color D.

Rnd 5: Ch 3, dc in same ch as joining and in next 7 dc; 2 dc in next dc; ch 12—*corner lp made*; *2 dc in next dc; dc in next 7 dc, 2 dc in next dc; ch 12—*corner lp made*; rep from * twice more; join in 3rd ch of beg ch-3. Change to Color B by drawing lp through; cut Color A.

Working in any corner, insert corner lp of Rnd 2 from back to front through corner lp of Rnd 1; insert corner lp of Rnd 3 from back to front through corner lp of Rnd 2; rep for corner lps on Rnds 4 and 5. Rep for rem corners.

Rnd 6: Ch 3, dc in same ch as joining and in next 9 dc; 2 dc in next dc; 5 hdc in next corner lp of Rnd 5—*hdc corner made*; *2 dc in next dc; dc in next 9 dc, 2 dc in next dc; 5 hdc in next corner lp of Rnd 5—*hdc corner made*; rep from * twice more; join in 3rd ch of beg ch-3.

Finish off and weave in all ends. ●

Square 82

Materials
- Yarn—Color A light yellow; Color B red; Color C turquoise

Pattern Stitches

Puff Stitch (puff st): Yo, draw up lp in st indicated, [yo, draw up lp in same st] twice; yo and draw through all 7 lps on hook—*puff st made*.

Large Puff Stitch (lg puff st): Yo, draw up lp in sp indicated, [yo, draw up lp in same st] 4 times; yo and draw through all 11 lps on hook—*lg puff st made*.

Beginning Cluster (beg CL): Ch 2, keeping last lp of each tr on hook, 2 tr in sp indicated; yo and draw through all 3 lps on hook—*beg CL made*.

Cluster (CL): Keeping last lp of each tr on hook, 3 tr in sp indicated; yo and draw through all 4 lps on hook—*CL made*.

Instructions

With Color A, ch 5; join to form a ring.

Rnd 1 (RS): Ch 1, 8 sc in ring; join in first sc.

Rnd 2: Ch 3 *(counts as a dc on this and following rnds)*, **puff st** *(see Pattern Stitches)* in same sc; [dc in next sc, puff st in same sc] 7 times; join in 3rd ch of beg ch-3—*8 puff sts*. Finish off Color A.

Rnd 3: Join Color B in sp between any dc and next puff st; ch 2, **lg puff st** *(see Pattern Stitches)* in same sp; ch 2, lg puff st in sp between same puff st and next dc; ch 2; *lg puff st in sp between dc and next puff st; ch 2, lg puff st between same puff st and next dc; ch 2; rep from * 6 times more; join in top of first puff st—*16 lg puff sts*. Finish off Color B.

Rnd 4: Join Color C in any ch-2 sp; in same sp work (**beg CL**—*see Pattern Stitches*, ch 3, **CL**—*see Pattern Stitches)*—*beg corner made*; 3 dc in next ch-2 sp; 3 hdc in next ch-2 sp; 3 dc in next ch-2 sp; *in next ch-2 sp work (CL, ch 3, CL)—*corner made*; 3 dc in next ch-2 sp; 3 hdc in next ch-2 sp; 3 dc in next ch-2 sp; rep from * twice more; join in top of beg CL.

Rnd 5: Ch 3, in next corner ch-3 sp work (dc, ch 3, dc)—*dc corner made*; *dc in next 11 sts, in next corner ch-3 sp work (dc, ch 3, dc)—*dc corner made*; rep from * twice more; dc in next 10 sts; join in 3rd ch of beg ch-3.

Rnd 6: Ch 3, dc in next dc, in next corner ch-3 sp work dc corner; *dc in next 13 dc, in next corner ch-3 sp work dc corner; rep from * twice more; dc in next 11 dc; join in 3rd ch of beg ch-3.

Rnd 7: Ch 1, sc in same ch as joining and in next 2 dc; 5 sc in next corner ch-3 sp—*sc corner made*; *sc in next 15 dc, 5 sc in next corner ch-3 sp—*sc corner made*; rep from * twice more; sc in next 12 dc; join in first sc.

Finish off and weave in all ends. ●

Square 83

Materials

- Yarn—Color A light purple; Color B dark purple; Color C yellow

Instructions

With Color A, ch 4; join to form a ring.

Rnd 1 (RS): Sl st in ring, ch 1, [sc in ring, ch 3] 8 times; join in first sc—*8 ch-3 sps*.

Rnd 2: Sl st in next ch-3 sp, ch 1, in same sp work (sc, hdc, 3 dc, hdc, sc)—*petal made*; *in next ch-3 sp work (sc, hdc, 3 dc, hdc, sc)—*petal made*; rep from * 6 times more; join in back of first sc on prev rnd—*8 petals*.

Rnd 3: Ch 5, working behind petals of prev rnd, [sl st in back of next sc on Rnd 1, ch 5] 7 times; join in joining sl st.

Rnd 4: In each ch-5 sp work (sc, hdc, 5 dc, hdc, sc)—*petal made*; join in back of joining sl st.

Rnd 5: Ch 7, working behind petals of prev rnd, [sl st in back of next sl st on Rnd 3, ch 7] 7 times; join in joining sl st.

Rnd 6: In each ch-7 sp work (sc, hdc, 7 dc, hdc, sc)—*petal made*; join in back of joining sl st.

Rnd 7: Ch 9, working behind petals of prev rnd, [sl st in back of next sl st on Rnd 5, ch 9] 7 times; join in joining sl st.

Rnd 8: In each ch-9 sp work (sc, hdc, 9 dc, hdc, sc)—*petal made*; join in back of joining sl st. Change to Color B by drawing lp through; cut Color A.

Rnd 9: Ch 1, working behind petals of prev rnd, sc in same sl st; ch 1; *in back of next sl st work (3 dc, ch 3, 3 dc)—*corner made*; ch 1, sc in back of next sl st; ch 1; rep from * twice more; in back of next sl st work (3 dc, ch 3, 3 dc)—*corner made*; ch 1; join in first sc. Finish off Color B.

Rnd 10: Join Color C in any corner ch-3 sp; ch 3, in same sp work (dc, ch 3, 2 dc)—*beg 2-dc corner made*; dc in next 3 dc, dc in next ch-1 sp, dc in next sc, dc in next ch-1 sp, dc in next 3 dc; *in next corner ch-3 sp work (2 dc, ch 3, 2 dc)—*2-dc corner made*; dc in next 3 dc, dc in next ch-1 sp, dc in next sc, dc in next ch-1 sp; dc in next 3 dc; rep from * twice more; join in 3rd ch of beg ch-3.

Rnd 11: Ch 3, dc in next dc, in next corner ch-3 sp work 2-dc corner; *dc in next 13 dc, in next corner ch-3 sp work 2-dc corner; rep from * twice more; dc in next 11 dc; join in 3rd ch of beg ch-3. Finish off Color C.

Rnd 12: Join Color B in any corner ch-3 sp; ch 1, 5 sc in same sp—*sc corner made*; sc in next 17 dc; *5 sc in next ch-3 sp—*sc corner made*; sc in next 17 dc; rep from * twice more; join in first sc.

Finish off and weave in all ends. ●

Square 84

Materials

- Yarn—Color A light purple; Color B dark purple; Color C yellow

Instructions

With Color A, ch 2.

Note: Rnds 1–7 are worked in continuous rnds. Do not join; mark beg of rnds.

Rnd 1 (RS): 4 sc in 2nd ch from hook.

Rnd 2: 3 sc in each sc—*12 sc.*

Rnd 3: *3 sc in next sc—*sc corner made*; sc in next 2 sc; rep from * 3 times more—*20 sc.*

Rnd 4: Sc in next sc, [sc corner in next sc, sc in next 4 sc] 3 times; sc corner in next sc; sc in next 3 sc—*28 sc.*

Rnd 5: Sc in next 2 sc, [sc corner in next sc, sc in next 6 sc] 3 times; sc corner in next sc; sc in next 4 sc—*36 sc.*

Rnd 6: Sc in next 3 sc, [sc corner in next sc, sc in next 8 sc] 3 times; sc corner in next sc; sc in next 5 sc—*44 sc.*

Rnd 7: Sc in next 4 sc, [sc corner in next sc, sc in next 10 sc] 3 times; sc corner in next sc; sc in next 6 sc, remove marker, sc in next 6 sc; join in first sc—*52 sc.* Finish off Color A.

Note: Remainder of square is worked in joined rnds.

Rnd 8: Join Color B in 2nd sc of any corner; ch 1, sc corner in same sc; sc in next 12 sc; *sc corner in next sc; sc in next 12 sc; rep from * twice more; join in first sc. Finish off Color B.

Rnd 9: Join Color C in 2nd sc of any corner; ch 3 *(counts as a dc)*, in same sc work (dc, ch 2, 2 dc)—*beg dc corner made*; ch 1, [sk next 2 sc, 2 dc in next sc, ch 1] 4 times; sk next 2 sc; *in next sc work (2 dc, ch 2, 2 dc)—*dc corner made*; ch 1, [sk next 2 sc, 2 dc in next sc, ch 1] 4 times; sk next 2 sc; rep from * twice more; join in 3rd ch of beg ch-3. Finish off Color C.

Rnd 10: Join Color B in ch-2 sp of any corner; ch 1, 3 sc in same sp—*sc corner made*; working in each dc and in each ch-1 sp, sc in next 17 sts; *3 sc in next corner ch-2 sp—*sc corner made*; sc in next 17 sts; rep from * twice more; join in first sc.

Rnd 11: Ch 1, sc in same sc as joining; sc corner in next sc; *sc in next 19 sc, sc corner in next sc; rep from * twice more; sc in next 18 sc; join in first sc.

Finish off and weave in all ends. ●

Square 85

Materials
- Yarn—Color A spring green; Color B emerald green

Instructions

Square
With Color A, ch 4; join to form a ring.

Rnd 1 (RS): Ch 3 *(counts as a dc on this and following rnds)*, 2 dc in ring; ch 3, [3 dc in ring, ch 3] 3 times; join in 3rd ch of beg ch-3.

Rnd 2: Sl st in next 2 dc and in next ch-3 sp, ch 3, in same sp work (2 dc, ch 3, 3 dc)—*beg corner made*; *in next ch-3 sp work (3 dc, ch 3, 3 dc)—*corner made*; rep from * twice more; join in 3rd ch of beg ch-3.

Rnd 3: Sl st in next 2 dc and in next ch-3 sp, beg corner in same sp; 3 dc in sp between next 2 3-dc groups; *in next corner ch-3 sp work corner; 3 dc in sp between next 2 3-dc groups; rep from * twice more; join in 3rd ch of beg ch-3. Finish off Color A.

Rnd 4: Join Color B in any ch-3 sp; beg corner in same sp; [3 dc in sp between next 2 3-dc groups] twice; *corner in next corner; [3 dc in sp between next 2 3-dc groups] twice; rep from * twice more; join in 3rd ch of beg ch-3.

Finish off and weave in all ends.

Shamrock

With Color B, ch 4; join to form a ring.

*Ch 3, 2 dc in ring; ch 3, sl st in ring; rep from * twice more; ch 9, sc in 2nd ch from hook and in next 7 chs; sl st in ring. Finish off, leaving a 12" end for sewing.

Finishing

Referring to photo for placement and with tapestry needle, tack Shamrock to Square. Weave in ends. ●

Square 86

Materials
- Yarn—Color A light gold; Color B red; Color C off white

Instructions

Flower

Center

With Color A, ch 5; join to form a ring.

Rnd 1 (RS): Ch 1, [sc in ring, ch 4] 8 times; join in first sc—*8 ch-4 sps*.

Rnd 2: Ch 2, working behind ch-4 sps on prev rnd, [sl st in next sc, ch 2] 7 times; join in joining sl st—*8 ch-2 sps*. Finish off Color A.

First Petal

Row 1: Join Color B in any ch-2 sp; ch 1, 4 sc in same sp. Ch 1, turn.

Row 2: 2 sc in next sc; sc in next 2 sc, 2 sc in next sc—*6 sc*. Ch 1, turn.

Row 3: Sc in each sc. Ch 1, turn.

Row 4: Rep Row 3.

Row 5: Sc in next 5 sc. Ch 1, turn, leaving last sc unworked.

Row 6: Sc in next 4 sc. Ch 1, turn, leaving last sc unworked.

Row 7: Sc in next 3 sc. Ch 1, turn, leaving last sc unworked.

Row 8: Sc in next 2 sc. Ch 1, turn, leaving last sc unworked.

Row 9: Sc in next sc, sl st in next sc; sl st in side of each row of petal to Rnd 2 of center; sl st in same ch-2 sp as petal just worked and in next ch-2 sp.

2nd–8th Petals

Row 1: Ch 1, 4 sc in same ch-2 sp as last sl st made. Ch 1, turn.

Rows 2–9: Rep Rows 2–9 of First Petal. At end of 8th Petal, do not work last sl st.

Finish off and weave in ends.

Square

Rnd 1 (RS): Working behind petals, join Color C in back of 4th sc on 2nd row of any petal; ch 3; *sl st in back of 4th sc on 2nd row of next petal, ch 3; rep from * 6 times more; join in joining sl st—*8 ch-3 sps.*

Rnd 2: Sl st in next ch-3 sp, ch 3 *(counts as a dc on this and following rnds)*, in same sp work (2 dc, ch 3, 3 dc)—*beg corner made*; 3 dc in next ch-3 sp; *in next ch-3 sp work (3 dc, ch 3, 3 dc)—*corner made*; 3 dc in next ch-3 sp; rep from * twice more; join in 3rd ch of beg ch-3.

Rnd 3: Ch 3, dc in next 2 dc, in next corner ch-3 sp work corner; *dc in next 9 dc, in next corner ch-3 sp work corner; rep from * twice more; dc in next 6 dc; join in 3rd ch of beg ch-3.

Rnd 4: Ch 3, dc in next 5 dc, corner in next corner; *dc in next 15 dc, corner in next corner; rep from * twice more; dc in next 9 dc; join in 3rd ch of beg ch-3.

Rnd 5: Ch 3, dc in next 8 dc, in next corner ch-3 sp work (2 dc, ch 2, 2 dc)—*2-dc corner made*; *dc in next 21 dc, in next corner ch-3 sp work (2 dc, ch 2, 2 dc)—*2-dc corner made*; rep from * twice more; dc in next 12 dc; join in 3rd ch of beg ch-3.

Finish off and weave in all ends.

Finishing

With tapestry needle and Color B, tack Petals to Square. ●

Square 87

Materials
- Yarn—Color A pink; Color B purple; Color C spring green

Pattern Stitches

Beginning Popcorn (beg PC): Ch 3, 3 dc in sp indicated; drop lp from hook, insert hook in 3rd ch of beg ch-3, draw dropped lp through—*beg PC made.*

Popcorn (PC): 4 dc in sp indicated; drop lp from hook, insert hook in first dc made, draw dropped lp through—*PC made.*

Instructions

With Color A, ch 6; join to form a ring.

Rnd 1 (RS): Beg PC *(see Pattern Stitches)* in ring; ch 4, [**PC** *(see Pattern Stitches)* in ring, ch 4] 3 times; join in top of beg PC—*4 ch-4 sps*. Finish off Color A.

Rnd 2: Join Color B in any ch-4 sp; in same sp work (beg PC, ch 4, PC)—*beg corner made*; ch 4; * in next ch-4 sp work (PC, ch 4, PC)—*corner made*; ch 4; rep from * twice more; join in top of beg PC. Finish off Color B.

Rnd 3: Join Color C in any corner ch-4 sp; ch 3 *(counts as a dc)*, in same sp work (2 dc, ch 3, 3 dc)—*beg dc corner made*; ch 1, 3 dc in next ch-4 sp; ch 1; *in next corner ch-4 sp work (3 dc, ch 3, 3 dc)—*dc corner made*; ch 1, 3 dc in next ch-4 sp; ch 1; rep from * twice more; join in 3rd ch of beg ch-3.

Finish off and weave in all ends. ●

Square 88

Materials
- Yarn—Color A pink; Color B spring green; Color C dark pink

Pattern Stitches
Beginning Puff Stitch (beg puff st): Ch 3, [yo, draw up lp in st indicated] twice; yo and draw through all 5 lps on hook—*beg puff st made.*

Puff Stitch (puff st): [Yo, draw up lp in st indicated] 3 times; yo and draw through all 7 lps on hook—*puff st made.*

Instructions
With Color A, ch 4; join to form a ring.

Rnd 1 (RS): Sl st in ring; ch 1, 8 sc in ring; join in first sc.

Rnd 2: Beg puff st *(see Pattern Stitches)* in next sc; ch 3, [**puff st** *(see Pattern Stitches)* in next sc, ch 3] 7 times; join in top of beg puff st—*8 puff sts.* Finish off Color A.

Rnd 3: Join Color B in any ch-3 sp; ch 3 *(counts as a dc on this and following rnds)*, in same sp work (2 dc, ch 2, 3 dc)—*beg corner made*; 3 dc in next ch-3 sp; *in next ch-3 sp work (3 dc, ch 2, 3 dc)—*corner made*; 3 dc in next ch-3 sp; rep from * twice more; join in 3rd ch of beg ch-3. Finish off Color B.

Rnd 4: Join Color C in any corner ch-2 sp; ch 1, 3 sc in same sp—*sc corner made*; sc in next 9 dc; *3 sc in next corner ch-2 sp—*sc corner made*; sc in next 9 dc; rep from * twice more; join in first sc.

Finish off and weave in all ends. ●

Square 89

Materials

- Yarn—Color A light pink; Color B purple; Color C dark pink

Instructions

Square

With Color A, ch 4; join to form a ring.

Rnd 1 (RS): Ch 1, 12 sc in ring; join in first sc.

Rnd 2: Ch 1, 3 sc in same sc—*corner made*; sc in next 2 sc; *3 sc in next sc—*corner made*; sc in next 2 sc; rep from * twice more; join in first sc.

Rnd 3: Ch 1, sc in same sc; corner in next sc; *sc in next 4 sc, corner in next sc; rep from * twice more; sc in next 3 sc; join in first sc.

Rnd 4: Ch 1, sc in same sc and in each sc to 2nd sc of next corner; corner in next sc; *sc in each sc to 2nd sc of next corner; corner in next sc; rep from * twice more; sc in each sc to first sc; join in first sc.

Rnds 5–14: Rep Rnd 4. Finish off Color A.

Zig Zag Chains

Note: Chains are worked on right side of Square.

Rnd 1: Join Color B around post *(see page 98)* of 2nd sc after any corner on Rnd 6; *ch 3, sl st around post of 2nd sc after same corner on Rnd 4; ch 3; on Rnd 6, sk next 3 sc, sl st around post of next sc; ch 3; on Rnd 4, sk next 2 sc, sl st around post of next sc; ch 3; on Rnd 6, sk next 3 sc, sl st around post of next sc; ch 4, sl st around post of 2nd sc after next corner; rep from * 3 times more, ending last rep without working last sl st; join around same post as yarn joining. Finish off Color B.

Rnd 2: Join Color C around post of 4th sc after any corner on Rnd 8; *ch 3; on Rnd 6, sl st around post of 2nd sc of next 3 unused sc; ch 3; on Rnd 8, sk next 3 sc, sl st around post of next sc**; rep from * to ** once more; ch 4; on Rnd 6, sl st around post of 2nd sc of next corner; ch 4; on Rnd 8, sl st around post of 4th sc after same corner; rep from * 3 times more, ending last rep without working last sl st; join around same post as yarn joining. Finish off Color C.

Rnd 3: Join Color B around post of 6th sc after any corner on Rnd 10; *ch 3; on Rnd 8, sl st around post of 2nd sc of next 3 unused sc; ch 3; on Rnd 10, sk next 3 sc, sl st around post of next sc**; rep from * to ** once more; ch 5; on Rnd 8, sl st around post of 2nd sc of next corner; ch 5; on Rnd 10, sl st around post of 6th sc after same corner; rep from * 3 times more, ending last rep without working last sl st; join around post of same sc as yarn joining.

Finish off and weave in all ends. ●

Square 90

Materials

- Yarn—Color A dark blue; Color B pale blue; Color C light blue

Pattern Stitch

Cluster (CL): Keeping last lp of each dc on hook, 3 dc in st indicated; yo and draw through all 4 lps on hook—*CL made*. Push CL to right side.

Instructions

With Color A, ch 4; join to form a ring.

Rnd 1 (WS): Ch 3 *(counts as a dc on this and following rnds)*, 11 dc in ring; join in 3rd ch of beg ch-3—*12 dc*. Change to Color B by drawing lp through; cut Color A. Ch 4 *(counts as first tr on following rnd)*, turn.

Rnd 2 (RS): Tr in same ch as joining; tr in sp between last dc and next dc, [2 tr in next dc, tr in sp between last dc and next dc] 11 times; join in 4th ch of turning ch-4—*36 tr*. Change to Color C by drawing lp through; cut Color B. Ch 1, turn.

Rnd 3: Sc in same ch as joining and in next tr; **CL** *(see Pattern Stitch)* in next tr; [sc in next 2 tr, CL in next tr] 11 times; join in first sc—*12 CLs*. Finish off Color C. Turn.

Rnd 4: Hold square with right side facing you; join Color B in first sc to left of any CL; ch 1, sc in same sc; hdc in next sc, dc in next CL, in next sc work (dc, ch 1, tr, ch 1, dc)—*corner made*; dc in next sc, hdc in next CL, sc in next 4 sts; *hdc in next sc, dc in next CL, in next sc work (dc, ch 1, tr, ch 1, dc)—*corner made*; dc in next sc, hdc in next CL**; sc in next 4 sts; rep from * once more, then rep from * to ** once; sc in next 3 sts; join in first sc.

Rnd 5: Ch 3, dc in next 3 sts, ch 2, sk next ch-1 sp, in next tr work corner; *ch 2, sk next ch-1 sp, dc in next 10 sts, ch 2, sk next ch-1 sp, in next tr work corner; rep from * twice more; ch 2, sk next ch-1 sp, dc in next 6 sts; join in 3rd ch of beg ch-3.

Finish off and weave in all ends. ●

Square 91

Materials
- Yarn—Color A light pink; Color B off white; Color C red; Color D dark green; Color E black

Instructions

Square
With Color D, ch 4; join to form a ring.

Rnd 1 (RS): Ch 1, [sc in ring, ch 4] 4 times; join in first sc.

Rnd 2: Sl st in next ch-4 sp, ch 3, in same sp work (2 dc, ch 3, 3 dc)—*beg corner made*; *in next ch-4 sp work (3 dc, ch 3, 3 dc)—*corner made*; rep from * twice more; join in 3rd ch of beg ch-3.

Rnd 3: Sl st in next 2 dc and in next corner ch-3 sp, beg corner in same sp; 3 dc in sp between next 2 3-dc groups; *in next corner ch-3 sp work corner; 3 dc in sp between next 2 3-dc groups; rep from * twice more; join in 3rd ch of beg ch-3.

Rnd 4: Sl st in next 2 dc and in next corner ch-3 sp, beg corner in same sp; [3 dc in sp between next 2 3-dc groups] twice; *corner in next corner; [3 dc in sp between next 2 3-dc groups] twice; rep from * twice more; join in 3rd ch of beg ch-3.

Rnd 5: Sl st in next 2 dc and in next corner ch-3 sp, beg corner in same sp; [3 dc in sp between next 2 3-dc groups] 3 times; * corner in next corner; [3 dc in sp between next 2 3-dc groups] 3 times; rep from * twice more; join in 3rd ch of beg ch-3. Finish off Color D.

Rnd 6: Join Color C in any corner ch-3 sp; ch 1, in same sp work (sc, ch 3, sc)—*sc corner made*; working in back lps only, sc in next 15 dc; *in next corner ch-3 sp work (sc, ch 3, sc)—*sc corner made*; sc in next 15 dc; rep from * twice more; join in first sc. Finish off Color C.

Rnd 7: Join Color D in any corner ch-3 sp; ch 1, 3 sc in same sp—*3-sc corner made*; working in back lps only, *sc in next 17 sc, 3 sc in next corner ch-3 sp—*3-sc corner made*; rep from * twice more; join in first sc.

Finish off and weave in ends.

Santa

Face
With Color A, ch 4; join to form a ring.

Rnd 1 (RS): Ch 3 *(counts as a dc on this and following rnds)*, 4 dc in ring; yo, draw up lp in ring, yo, draw through 2 lps on hook; drop Color A, draw Color B through both lps on hook; carrying Color A behind work and working over it with Color B, 6 dc in ring for beard; drop Color B; join in 3rd ch of beg ch-3 by drawing Color A through.

Rnd 2: Continuing with Color A and carrying Color B as before, ch 1, 2 sc in same ch and in each of next 5 dc; change to Color B by drawing lp through; drop Color A; 2 sc in each of next 6 dc; join in first sc. Cut Color A.

Beard and Hat Trim

Rnd 3: Ch 5, turn; sl st in next sc, [ch 5, sl st in next sc] 11 times; sl st in next sc, sk next sc, sc in next 8 sc, sk next sc, sl st in next sc. Finish off Color B, leaving a 12" end for sewing.

Hat

With RS facing you, join Color C in back lp of last sc of Rnd 3.

Row 1: Ch 2 *(counts as an hdc)*, working in back lps only, dc in next 6 sc, hdc in next sc. Ch 1, turn.

Row 2: Sc in next hdc, hdc in next 6 dc, sc in next hdc. Ch 1, turn.

Row 3: Sk next sc, dec over next 2 hdc *(to work dec: draw up lp in each of next 2 sts, yo and draw through all 3 lps on hook—dec made)*; sc in next 2 hdc, dec as before over next 2 hdc—*4 sc*. Ch 1, turn.

Row 4: Sk next sc, dec; sl st in next sc. Finish off Color C, leaving a 12" end for sewing.

Row 5: With RS facing you, join Color B in sc on Row 4; ch 2, in same st work (dc, ch 2, sl st). Finish off, leaving an 8" end for sewing.

Finishing

Referring to photo for placement and with tapestry needle and Color E, make one cross st for each eye. With corresponding color yarn, tack Santa to center of Square. Weave. ●

Square 92

Materials

- Yarn—Color A gray; Color B spring green; Color C black

Instructions

Square

With Color A, ch 4; join to form a ring.

Rnd 1 (RS): Ch 3 *(counts as a dc on this and following rnds)*, 2 dc in ring; ch 2, [3 dc in ring, ch 2] 3 times; join in 3rd ch of beg ch-3—*4 ch-2 sps*.

Rnd 2: Sl st in next 2 dc and in next ch-2 sp, ch 3, in same sp work (2 dc, ch 2, 3 dc)—*beg corner made*; ch 1; *in next ch-2 sp work (3 dc, ch 2, 3 dc)—*corner made*; ch 1; rep from * twice more; join in 3rd ch of beg ch-3.

Rnd 3: Sl st in next 2 dc and in next ch-2 sp, beg corner in same sp; ch 1, 3 dc in next ch-1 sp; ch 1; *in next corner ch-2 sp work corner; ch 1, 3 dc in next ch-1 sp; ch 1; rep from * twice more; join in 3rd ch of beg ch-3.

Rnd 4: Sl st in next 2 dc and in next ch-2 sp, beg corner in same sp; ch 1, [3 dc in next ch-1 sp, ch 1] twice; *corner in next corner; ch 1, [3 dc in next ch-1 sp, ch 1] twice; rep from * twice more; join in 3rd ch of beg ch-3. Finish off Color A.

Rnd 5: Join Color B in any corner ch-2 sp; beg corner in same sp; ch 1, [3 dc in next ch-1 sp, ch 1] 3 times; *corner in next corner; ch 1, [3 dc in next ch-1 sp, ch 1] 3 times; rep from * twice more; join in 3rd ch of beg ch-3. Finish off Color B.

Rnd 6: Join Color C in any corner ch-2 sp; ch 1, 3 sc in same sp—*sc corner made*; working in each dc and in each ch-1 sp, sc in next 19 sts; *3 sc in next corner ch-2 sp—*sc corner made*; sc in next 19 sts; rep from * twice more; join in first sc.

Finish off and weave in all ends.

Cat

Body
With Color C, ch 23.

Row 1 (RS): Sl st in 3rd ch from hook and in next 3 chs; sc in next 6 chs, hdc in next ch—*tail made*; sc in next 10 chs. Ch 1, turn.

Row 2: Sc in next 10 sc. Ch 1, turn.

Rows 3–10: Rep Row 2.

Row 11: Sc in next sc, dec over next 2 sc *(to work dec: draw up lp in each of next 2 sc, yo and draw through all 3 lps on hook—dec made)*; sc in next 4 sc, dec as before over next 2 sc; sc in next sc—*8 sc*. Ch 1, turn.

Row 12: Sc in next sc, dec; sc in next 2 sc, dec; sc in next sc—*6 sc*. Ch 1, turn.

Row 13: Sc in each sc. Finish off Color C. Set aside.

Head
With Color C, ch 3.

Rnd 1 (RS): 10 sc in 2nd ch from hook; join in first sc.

Rnd 2: Ch 1, 2 sc in same sc and in each rem sc; join in first sc—*20 sc*.

Rnd 3: Ch 1, sc in same sc and in each rem sc; join in first sc.

Rnd 4: Ch 1, in same sc work (sc, ch 5, sc)—*ear made*; sc in next 4 sc, in next sc work (sc, ch 5, sc)—*ear made*; sc in next 14 sc; join in first sc.

Finish off and weave in ends.

Finishing
Hold Head with right side facing you. With tapestry needle and Color B, embroider eyes with two slanted straight stitches as shown in photo. With Color A, embroider whiskers.

Referring to photo for placement, sew Cat body to Square. Place head on top of body, covering Rows 12 and 13; sew in place. ●

Square 93

Materials
• Yarn—Color A black; Color B red; Color C off white

Instructions

Flower

Center
With Color A, ch 2.

Rnd 1 (RS): 6 sc in 2nd ch from hook; join in first sc.

Rnd 2: Ch 1, 2 sc in same sc and in each rem sc; join in first sc—*12 sc*.

Rnd 3: Ch 8, [sl st in next sc, ch 8] 11 times; join in joining sl st—*12 ch-8 sps*. Finish off, leaving a 12" end for sewing.

Petals
With Color B, ch 6; join to form a ring.

Rnd 1 (RS): Ch 1, [sc in ring, ch 5] 5 times; join in first sc—*5 ch-5 sps*.

Rnd 2: *Sl st in next ch-5 sp, in same sp work (ch 4, 10 tr, ch 4, sl st)—*petal made*; rep from * 4 times more; join in joining sl st—*5 petals*.

Rnd 3: *Sl st in next 4 chs of next ch-4 *(along side of next petal)*; ch 3, dc in next 10 tr, ch 3, sl st in next 4 chs of next ch-4 *(down side of same petal)*; rep from * 4 times more; sl st in first sl st. Finish off, leaving a 12" end for sewing.

Square
With Color C, ch 4; join to form a ring.

Rnd 1 (RS): Ch 1, 8 sc in ring; join in first sc.

Rnd 2: Ch 1, 2 sc in same sc and in each rem sc; join in first sc—*16 sc*.

Rnd 3: Ch 4 *(counts as a dc and a ch-1 sp on this and following rnd)*, [dc in next sc, ch 1] 15 times; join in 3rd ch of beg ch-4.

Rnd 4: Ch 4, dc in next ch-1 sp, ch 1, [dc in next dc, ch 1, dc in next ch-1 sp, ch 1] 15 times; join in 3rd ch of beg ch-4—*32 dc*.

Rnd 5: Sl st in next ch-1 sp, ch 4 *(counts as a tr)*, in same sp work (tr, ch 2, 2 tr)—*beg corner made*; tr in next ch-1 sp, [dc in next ch-1 sp, ch 1] 4 times; dc in next ch-1 sp, tr in next ch-1 sp; *in next ch-1 sp work (2 tr, ch 2, 2 tr)—*corner made*; tr in next ch-1 sp, [dc in next ch-1 sp, ch 1] 4 times; dc in next ch-1 sp, tr in next ch-1 sp; rep from * twice more; join in 4th ch of beg ch-4.

Rnd 6: Ch 3 *(counts as a dc)*, dc in next tr, in next corner ch-2 sp work (2 dc, ch 2, 2 dc)—*dc corner made*; *dc in next 3 tr, in next dc, and in next ch-1 sp, [ch 1, dc in next ch-1 sp] 3 times; dc in next dc and in next 3 tr, in next corner ch-2 sp work (2 dc, ch 2, 2 dc)—*dc corner made*; rep from * twice more; dc in next 3 tr, in next dc and next ch-1 sp, [ch 1, dc in next ch-1 sp] 3 times; dc in next dc and next tr; join in 3rd ch of beg ch-3.

Rnd 7: Ch 1, sc in same ch as joining and in next 3 dc, 3 sc in next corner ch-2 sp—*sc corner made*; working in each dc and in each ch-1 sp, *sc in next 19 sts, 3 sc in next corner ch-2 sp—*sc corner made*; rep from * twice more; sc in next 15 sts; join in first sc.

Finish off and weave in ends.

Finishing
With tapestry needle, tack Petals to Square. Tack Flower Center to center of Petals. Weave in all ends. ●

Square 94

Materials
- Yarn—Color A yellow; Color B dark pink; Color C light pink; Color D dark green

Pattern Stitches

Beginning Popcorn (beg PC): Ch 3, 3 dc in ring; drop lp from hook, insert hook in 3rd ch of beg ch-3, draw dropped lp through—*beg PC made*.

Popcorn (PC): 4 dc in ring; drop lp from hook, insert hook in first dc, draw dropped lp through—*PC made*.

Back Post Slip Stitch (bpslst): Insert hook from back to front to back around post *(see page 98)* of st indicated, yo, draw around stitch and through lp on hook—*bpslst made*.

Instructions
With Color A, ch 4; join to form a ring.

Rnd 1 (RS): Beg PC *(see Pattern Stitches)* in ring; ch 3, [**PC** *(see Pattern Stitches)* in ring, ch 3] 3 times; join in top of beg PC—*4 ch-3 sps*. Finish off Color A.

Rnd 2: Join Color B in any ch-3 sp; ch 4, [sl st in next ch-3 sp, ch 4] 3 times; join in joining sl st—*4 ch-4 sps*.

Rnd 3: Sl st in next ch-4 sp, ch 1, in same sp work (sc, hdc, 5 dc, hdc, sc)—*petal made*; in each rem ch-4 sp work (sc, hdc, 5 dc, hdc, sc)—*petal made—4 petals*; do not join.

Rnd 4: *Bpslst *(see Pattern Stitches)* around first sc of next petal; ch 4, sk next 3 sts, bpslst around next st of same petal; ch 4; rep from * 3 times; join in first sl st—*8 ch-4 sps*. Finish off Color B.

Rnd 5: Join Color C in any ch-4 sp; ch 1, in same sp work (sc, hdc, 3 dc, hdc, sc)—*petal made*; in each rem ch-4 sp work (sc, hdc, 3 dc, hdc, sc)—*petal made—8 petals*; do not join.

Rnd 6: *Bpslst around post of first sc of next petal; ch 3; rep from * 7 times more; join in first sl st—*8 ch-3 sps*. Finish off Color C.

Rnd 7: Join Color D in any ch-3 sp; ch 1, in same sp work (2 sc, 2 hdc, dc); ch 3—*corner sp made*; in next ch-3 sp work (dc, 2 hdc, 2 sc); *in next ch-3 sp work (2 sc, 2 hdc, dc); ch 3—*corner sp made*; in next ch-3 sp work (dc, 2 hdc, 2 sc); rep from * twice more; join in first sc.

Rnd 8: Ch 1, sc in same sc and in next 4 sts; 5 sc in next corner ch-3 sp—*sc corner made*; *sc in next 10 sts, 5 sc in next corner ch-3 sp—*sc corner made*; rep from * twice more; sc in next 5 sts; join in first sc.

Finish off and weave in all ends. ●

Square 95

Materials
- Yarn—Color A light pink; Color B dark green; Color C yellow

Pattern Stitch
Popcorn (PC): 5 dc in sp indicated; drop lp from hook, insert hook in first dc, draw dropped lp through—*PC made*.

Instructions
With Color A, ch 4; join to form a ring.

Rnd 1 (RS): Ch 3 *(counts as a dc on this and following rnds)*, 3 dc in ring; ch 1, [4 dc in ring, ch 1] 3 times; join in 3rd ch of beg ch-3—*4 ch-1 sps*. Finish off Color A.

Rnd 2: Join Color B in any ch-1 sp; ch 3, in same sp work (3 dc, ch 1, 4 dc)—*beg corner made*; ch 1; *in next ch-1 sp work (4 dc, ch 1, 4 dc)—*corner made*; ch 1; rep from * twice more; join in 3rd ch of beg ch-3. Finish off Color B.

Rnd 3: Join Color C in any corner ch-1 sp; ch 3, in same sp work (dc, **PC**—*see Pattern Stitch*, 2 dc)—*beg PC corner made*; sk next dc, dc in next 3 dc, PC in next ch-1 sp; sk next dc, dc in next 3 dc; *in next corner ch-1 sp work (2 dc, PC, 2 dc)—*PC corner made*; sk next dc, dc in next 3 dc, PC in next ch-1 sp; sk next dc, dc in next 3 dc; rep from * twice more; join in 3rd ch of beg ch-3. Finish off Color C.

Rnd 4: Join Color B in top of any corner PC; ch 1, 3 sc in same PC—*sc corner made*; sc in next 5 dc, in top of next PC, and in next 5 dc; *3 sc in top of next PC—*sc corner made*; sc in next 5 dc, in top of next PC, and in next 5 dc; rep from * twice more; join in first sc.

Finish off and weave in all ends. ●

Square 96

Materials
- Yarn—Color A off white; Color B dark red

Instructions
With Color A, ch 6; join to form a ring.

Rnd 1 (RS): Ch 3 *(counts as a dc on this and following rnds)*, 15 dc in ring; join in 3rd ch of beg ch-3—*16 dc*.

Rnd 2: Ch 5 *(counts as a dc and a ch-2 sp)*, dc in same ch; sk next dc; *in next dc work (dc, ch 2, dc); sk next dc; rep from * 6 times more; join in 3rd ch of beg ch-5—*8 ch-2 sps.*

Rnd 3: Sl st in next ch-2 sp, ch 3, in same sp work (dc, ch 3, 2 dc); in each rem ch-2 sp work (2 dc, ch 3, 2 dc); join in 3rd ch of beg ch-3—*8 ch-3 sps.*

Rnd 4: Sl st in next dc and in next ch-3 sp, ch 3, in same sp work (2 dc, ch 3, 3 dc); in each rem ch-3 sp work (3 dc, ch 3, 3 dc); join in 3rd ch of beg ch-3.

Rnd 5: Sl st in next 2 dc and in next ch-3 sp, ch 3, in same sp work (3 dc, ch 2, 4 dc); in each rem ch-3 sp work (4 dc, ch 2, 4 dc); join in 3rd ch of beg ch-3—*8 ch-2 sps.* Finish off Color A.

Rnd 6: Join Color B in any ch-2 sp; ch 3, in same sp work (dc, ch 3, 2 dc)—*beg corner made*; working in sps between dc, dc in next 5 sps, hdc in next sp, sc in next sp, sl st in next ch-2 sp; sc in next sp, hdc in next sp, dc in next 5 sps; *in next ch-2 sp work (2 dc, ch 3, 2 dc)—*corner made*; dc in next 5 sps, hdc in next sp, sc in next sp, sl st in next ch-2 sp; sc in next sp, hdc in next sp, dc in next 5 sps; rep from * twice more; join in 3rd ch of beg ch-3.

Rnd 7: Ch 3, dc in next dc, in next corner ch-3 sp work corner; *dc in next 6 dc, sc in next 7 sts, dc in next 6 dc, in next corner ch-3 sp work corner; rep from * twice more; dc in next 6 dc, sc in next 7 sts, dc in next 4 dc; join in 3rd ch of beg ch-3.

Rnd 8: Ch 1, sc in same sc and in next 3 dc; 3 sc in next corner ch-3 sp—*sc corner made*; *sc in next 23 sts, 3 sc in next ch-3 sp—sc corner made; rep from * twice more; sc in next 19 sts; join in first sc.

Finish off and weave in all ends. ●

Square 97

Materials
- Yarn—Color A off white; Color B dark blue; Color C light blue

Pattern Stitch
Double Triple Crochet (dtr): Yo 3 times, draw up lp in st indicated, [yo, draw through 2 lps on hook] 4 times—*dtr made.*

Instructions
With Color A, ch 5; join to form a ring.

Rnd 1 (RS): Ch 1, [3 sc in ring, ch 2] 4 times; join in first sc—*12 sc.* Finish off Color A.

Rnd 2: Join Color B in any ch-2 sp; ch 1, in same sp work (sc, ch 2, sc)—*corner made*; *sc in front lp of next sc, ch 17, sk next sc, sc in front lp of next sc, in next ch-2 sp work (sc, ch 2, sc)—*corner made*; rep from * 3 times more, ending last rep without working last corner; join in first sc—*4 ch-17 sps.*

Rnd 3: Sl st in next corner ch-2 sp, ch 5 *(counts as a dc and a ch-2 sp)*, dc in same sp—*beg dc corner made*; *sc in next 6 chs of next ch-17 sp, ch 2, sc in next 2 chs; in next ch work (dc, ch 2, dc); sc in next 2 chs, ch 2, sc in next 6 chs; in next corner ch-2 sp work (dc, ch 2, dc)—*dc corner made*; rep from * 3 times more, ending last rep without working last corner; join in 3rd ch of beg ch-5. Finish off Color B.

Rnd 4: Working behind ch-17 sps in skipped sc and unused lps of Rnd 1, join Color C in back lp of any skipped sc of Rnd 1; ch 3 *(counts as a dc on this and following rnds)*, dc in next unused lp, ch 3; *dc in next unused lp, in back lp of next sc, and in next unused lp; ch 3; rep from * twice more; dc in next unused lp; join in 3rd ch of beg ch-3.

Rnd 5: Sl st in next dc and in next ch-3 sp, ch 3, in same sp work (2 dc, ch 2, 3 dc)—*beg 3-dc corner made*; ch 2; *in next ch-3 sp work (3 dc, ch 2, 3 dc)—*3-dc corner made*; ch 2; rep from * twice more; join in 3rd ch of beg ch-3.

Rnd 6: Sl st in next 2 dc and in next corner ch-2 sp, beg 3-dc corner in same sp; ch 2, 3 dc in next ch-2 sp; ch 2; *in next corner ch-2 sp work 3-dc corner; ch 2, 3 dc in next ch-2 sp; ch 2; rep from * twice more; join in 3rd ch of beg ch-3. Finish off Color C.

Rnd 7: Join Color A in any corner ch-2 sp; ch 1, sc in same sp; *dtr *(see Pattern Stitch)* in corresponding corner ch-2 sp on Rnd 3; on working rnd, sc in same corner ch-2 sp as last sc made, [sc in next 3 dc, 2 sc in next ch-2 sp] twice; sc in next 3 dc, sc in next corner ch-2 sp; rep from * 3 times more, ending last rep without working last sc; join in first sc. Finish off Color A.

Rnd 8: Join Color C in any dtr; beg dc corner in same dtr; dc in next 15 sc, [dc corner in next dtr, dc in next 15 sc] 3 times; join in 3rd ch of beg ch-5.

Rnd 9: Sl st in next corner ch-2 sp; beg dc corner in same sp; *dc in next 7 dc, 3 sc in ch-2 sp at tip of next ch-17 sp on Rnd 3; on working rnd, sk next 3 dc, dc in next 7 dc, dc corner in next dc corner; rep from * 3

times more, ending last rep without working last dc corner; join in 3rd ch of beg ch-5. Finish off Color C.

Rnd 10: Join Color A in any corner ch-2 sp; ch 1, 3 sc in same sp—*sc corner made*; sc in next 19 sc; *3 sc in next corner ch-2 sp—*sc corner made*; sc in next 19 sc; rep from * twice more; join in first sc.

Finish off and weave in all ends. ●

Square 98

Materials
- Yarn—Color pink

Pattern Stitches
Beginning Cluster (beg CL): Ch 2, yo, draw up lp in ring, [yo, draw through 2 lps on hook] twice—*beg CL made*.

Cluster (CL): Keeping last lp of each dc on hook, 2 dc in ring; yo and draw through all 3 lps on hook—*CL made*.

Instructions

Ch 5, join to form a ring.

Rnd 1 (RS): Beg CL *(see Pattern Stitches)* in ring; ch 2, [**CL** *(see Pattern Stitches)* in ring, ch 2] 7 times; join in top of beg CL—*8 CLs*.

Rnd 2: Sl st in next ch-2 sp, ch 1, in same sp work (sc, ch 9, sc); ch 4, sc in next ch-2 sp, ch 4; *in next ch-2 sp work (sc, ch 9, sc); ch 4, sc in next ch-2 sp, ch 4; rep from * twice more; join in first sc.

Rnd 3: Sl st in next ch-9 sp, ch 3 *(counts as a dc on this and following rnds)*, in same sp work (8 dc, ch 2, 9 dc)—*beg petal made*; sc in next ch-4 sp, ch 9, sc in next ch-4 sp; *in next ch-9 sp work (9 dc, ch 2, 9 dc)—*petal made*; sc in next ch-4 sp, ch 9, sc in next ch-4 sp; rep from * twice more; join in 3rd ch of beg ch-3—*4 petals*.

Rnd 4: Sl st in next 4 dc; ch 4, in next ch-2 sp work (sc, ch 3, sc)—*corner made*; *ch 4, sk next 4 dc, sl st in next dc, ch 4, sl st in 5th ch of next ch-9 sp, ch 4, sk next 4 dc of next petal, sl st in next dc, ch 4, in next ch-2 sp work (sc, ch 3, sc)—*corner made*; rep from * twice more; ch 4, sk next 4 dc, sl st in next dc, ch 4, sl st in 5th ch of next ch-9 sp, ch 4; join in 4th sl st of beg 4 sl sts.

Rnd 5: Sl st in next ch of next ch-4 sp and in same sp, ch 3, 3 dc in same sp; in next corner ch-3 sp work (2 dc, ch 3, 2 dc)—*dc corner made*; *4 dc in each of next 4 ch-3 sps; in next corner ch-3 sp work (2 dc, ch 3, 2 dc)—*dc corner made*; rep from * twice more; 4 dc in each of next 3 ch-3 sps; join in 3rd ch of beg ch-3.

Rnd 6: Ch 1, sc in same ch and in next 5 dc; 3 sc in next corner ch-3 sp—*sc corner made*; *sc in next 20 dc, 3 sc in next corner ch-3 sp—*sc corner made*; rep from * twice more; sc in next 14 dc; join in first sc.

Finish off and weave in ends. ●

Square 99

Materials

- Yarn—Color A dark brown; Color B brown; Color C off white

Instructions

Starting with Color A for nose, ch 4; join to form a ring.

Rnd 1 (RS): Ch 3 *(counts as a dc on this and following rnds)*, 7 dc in ring; join in 3rd ch of beg ch-3—*8 dc*. Change to Color B by drawing lp through; cut Color A.

Rnd 2: Ch 1, sc in same ch; working in back lps only, sc in each dc; join in back lp of first sc. Push nose to right side.

Rnd 3: Ch 3, dc in same sc; working in back lps only, 3 dc in next sc; [2 dc in next sc, 3 dc in next sc] 3 times; join in 3rd ch of beg ch-3—*20 dc*.

Rnd 4: Ch 3, dc in same ch; 2 dc in each rem dc; join in 3rd ch of beg ch-3—*40 dc*.

Rnd 5: Working in front lps only, in next dc work (sl st, ch 2, 8 dc, ch 2, sl st)—*ear made*; sc in next 9 dc, in next dc work (sl st, ch 2, 8 dc, ch 2, sl st)—*ear made*; sc in next 29 dc; join in first sl st. Finish off Color B.

Rnd 6: Join Color C in unused lp of Rnd 4 behind first ear; ch 3, in same lp work (2 dc, ch 3, 3 dc)—*beg corner made*; working in rem unused lps of Rnd 4, dc in next 9 lps, in unused lp behind next ear work (3 dc, ch 3, 3 dc)—*corner made*; dc in next 9 lps; *in next dc work (3 dc, ch 3, 3 dc)—*corner made*; dc in next 9 lps; rep from * once more; join in 3rd ch of beg ch-3. Finish off Color C.

Rnd 7: Join Color A in any corner ch-3 sp; ch 1, 3 sc in same sp—*sc corner made*; sc in next 15 dc; *3 sc in next corner ch-3 sp—*sc corner made*; sc in next 15 dc; rep from * twice more; join in first sc. Finish off Color A.

Rnd 8: Join Color C in 2nd sc of any corner; ch 1, in same sc work (sc, ch 1, sc)—*ch-1 corner made*; *sc in next 17 sc, in next sc work (sc, ch 1, sc)—*ch-1 corner made*; rep from * twice more; sc in next 17 sc; join in first sc.

Finish off and weave in all ends.

Finishing
Referring to photo for placement and with tapestry needle and double strand of Color A, embroider mouth and eyes using straight stitches. ●

Square 100

Materials
- Yarn—Color A blue; Color B pale blue; Color C dark blue

Pattern Stitches
Beginning Cluster (beg CL): Ch 2, keeping last lp of each dc on hook, 2 dc in st indicated; yo and draw through all 3 lps on hook—*beg CL made*.

Cluster (CL): Keeping last lp of each dc on hook, 3 dc in st indicated; yo and draw through all 4 lps on hook—*CL made*.

Triple Crochet Cluster (tr CL): Keeping last lp of each tr on hook, 3 tr in sp indicated; yo and draw through all 4 lps on hook—*tr CL made*.

Double Triple Crochet (dtr): Yo 3 times, draw up lp in st indicated, [yo, draw through 2 lps on hook] 4 times—*dtr made*.

Double Triple Crochet Cluster (dtr CL): Keeping last lp of each dtr on hook, 3 dtr in st indicated; yo and draw through all 4 lps on hook—*dtr CL made*.

Instructions

With Color A, ch 6; join to form a ring.

Note: *Rnds 1–5 are worked in continuous rnds. Do not join; mark beg of rnds.*

Rnd 1 (RS): Ch 1, [sc in ring, ch 5] 8 times.

Rnd 2: *In next ch-5 sp work (sc, hdc, dc, hdc, sc)— *petal made*; rep from * 7 times more—*8 petals.*

Rnd 3: Working behind petals of prev rnd, [sc in back of next sc on Rnd 1, ch 4] 8 times—*8 ch-4 sps.*

Rnd 4: *In next ch-4 sp work (sc, hdc, 3 dc, hdc, sc)— *petal made*; rep from * 7 times more—*8 petals.*

Rnd 5: Working behind petals of prev rnd, [sc in back of next sc on Rnd 3, ch 4] 8 times—*8 ch-4 sps.*

Rnd 6: *In each ch-4 sp work (sc, hdc, 5 dc, hdc, sc)— *petal made*; rep from * 7 times more; join in first sc—*8 petals*. Finish off Color A.

Rnd 7: Join Color B in 3rd dc of any petal; in same dc work (**beg CL**—*see Pattern Stitches*, ch 2, **CL**—*see Pattern Stitches*); ch 3, in 3rd dc of next petal work (**tr CL**—*see Pattern Stitches*, ch 4, **dtr CL**—*see Pattern Stitches*, ch 4, tr CL)—*corner made*; ch 3; *in 3rd dc of next petal work (CL, ch 2, CL); ch 3, in 3rd dc of next petal work (tr CL, ch 4, dtr CL, ch 4, tr CL)—*corner made*; ch 3; rep from * twice more; join in top of beg CL. Finish off Color B.

Rnd 8: Join Color C in top of any dtr CL; ch 3, in same sp work (2 dc, ch 3, 3 dc)—*beg dc corner made*; 3 dc in next ch-4 sp; 3 dc in next ch-3 sp; 3 dc in next ch-2 sp; 3 dc in next ch-3 sp; 3 dc in next ch-4 sp; *in top of next dtr CL work (3 dc, ch 3, 3 dc)—*dc corner made*; 3 dc in next ch-4 sp; 3 dc in next ch-3 sp; 3 dc in next ch-2 sp; 3 dc in next ch-3 sp; 3 dc in next ch-4 sp; rep from * twice more; join in 3rd ch of beg ch-3.

Rnd 9: Ch 3 *(counts as a dc)*, dc in next 2 dc; *in next corner ch-3 sp work dc corner; dc in next 21 dc; rep from * twice more; in next corner ch-3 sp work dc corner; dc in next 18 dc; join in 3rd ch of beg ch-3. Finish off Color C.

Rnd 10: Join Color A in any corner ch-3 sp; ch 1, 3 sc in same sp—*sc corner made*; sc in next 27 dc; *3 sc in next corner ch-3 sp—*corner made*; sc in next 27 sc; rep from * twice more; join in first sc.

Finish off and weave in all ends. ●

Square 101

Materials

- Yarn—Color A dark turquoise; Color B red; Color C off white

Pattern Stitch

Cluster (CL): Keeping last lp of each dc on hook, 3 dc in st indicated; yo and draw through all 4 lps on hook—*CL made*. Push CL to right side.

Instructions

With Color A, ch 4; join to form a ring.

Rnd 1 (WS): Ch 3 *(counts as a dc on this and following rnds)*, 11 dc in ring; join in 3rd ch of beg ch-3—*12 dc*. Change to Color B by drawing lp through; cut Color A. Ch 4 *(counts as a tr on this and following rnds)*, turn.

Rnd 2 (RS): Tr in same ch as joining; tr in sp between last dc and next dc, [2 tr in next dc, tr in sp between last dc and next dc] 11 times; join in 4th ch of turning ch-4—*36 tr*. Change to Color A by drawing lp through; cut Color B. Ch 1, turn.

Rnd 3: Sc in same ch as joining and in next tr; **CL** *(see Pattern Stitch)* in next tr; [sc in next 2 tr, CL in next tr] 11 times; join in first sc—*12 CLs*. Finish off Color A.

Rnd 4: With right side facing you, join Color C in first sc after any CL; ch 1, sc in same sc; hdc in next sc, dc in next CL; *in next sc work (dc, ch 1, tr, ch 1, dc)—*corner made*; dc in next sc, hdc in next CL, sc in next 4 sts, hdc in next sc, dc in next CL; rep from * twice more; in next sc work (dc, ch 1, tr, ch 1, dc)—*corner made*; dc in next sc, hdc in next CL, sc in next 3 sts; join in first sc.

Rnd 5: Ch 3, dc in next 3 sts, ch 2, sk next ch-1 sp; *corner in next tr; ch 2, sk next ch-1 sp, dc in next 10 sts, ch 2, sk next ch-1 sp; rep from * twice more; corner in next tr; ch 2, sk next ch-1 sp, dc in next 6 sts; join in 3rd ch of beg ch-3.

Rnd 6: Ch 3, dc in next 3 dc, ch 2, sk next dc; *in next tr work (dc, ch 2, tr, ch 2, dc)—*tr corner made*; ch 2, sk next dc, dc in next 10 dc, ch 2, sk next dc; rep from * twice more; in next tr work (dc, ch 2, tr, ch 2, dc)—*tr corner made*; ch 2, sk next dc, dc in next 6 dc; join in 3rd ch of beg ch-3. Finish off Color C.

Rnd 7: Join Color A in any corner tr; ch 1, 3 sc in same tr—*sc corner made*; 2 sc in next ch-2 sp; sc in next dc, 2 sc in next ch-2 sp; sc in next 10 dc, 2 sc in next ch-2 sp; sc in next dc, 2 sc in next ch-2 sp; *3 sc in next tr—*sc corner made*; 2 sc in next ch-2 sp; sc in next dc, 2 sc in next ch-2 sp; sc in next 10 dc, 2 sc in next ch-2 sp; sc in next dc, 2 sc in next ch-2 sp; rep from * twice more; join in first sc.

Finish off and weave in all ends. ●

Metric Conversion Charts

METRIC CONVERSIONS

yards	x	.9144	=	metres (m)
yards	x	91.44	=	centimetres (cm)
inches	x	2.54	=	centimetres (cm)
inches	x	25.40	=	millimetres (mm)
inches	x	.0254	=	metres (m)

centimetres	x	.3937	=	inches
metres	x	1.0936	=	yards

INCHES INTO MILLIMETRES & CENTIMETRES (Rounded off slightly)

inches	mm	cm	inches	cm	inches	cm	inches	cm
1/8	3	0.3	5	12.5	21	53.5	38	96.5
1/4	6	0.6	5 1/2	14	22	56	39	99
3/8	10	1	6	15	23	58.5	40	101.5
1/2	13	1.3	7	18	24	61	41	104
5/8	15	1.5	8	20.5	25	63.5	42	106.5
3/4	20	2	9	23	26	66	43	109
7/8	22	2.2	10	25.5	27	68.5	44	112
1	25	2.5	11	28	28	71	45	114.5
1 1/4	32	3.2	12	30.5	29	73.5	46	117
1 1/2	38	3.8	13	33	30	76	47	119.5
1 3/4	45	4.5	14	35.5	31	79	48	122
2	50	5	15	38	32	81.5	49	124.5
2 1/2	65	6.5	16	40.5	33	84	50	127
3	75	7.5	17	43	34	86.5		
3 1/2	90	9	18	46	35	89		
4	100	10	19	48.5	36	91.5		
4 1/2	115	11.5	20	51	37	94		

KNITTING NEEDLES CONVERSION CHART

Canada/U.S.	0	1	2	3	4	5	6	7	8	9	10	10½	11	13	15
Metric (mm)	2	2¼	2¾	3¼	3½	3¾	4	4½	5	5½	6	6½	8	9	10

CROCHET HOOKS CONVERSION CHART

Canada/U.S.	1/B	2/C	3/D	4/E	5/F	6/G	8/H	9/I	10/J	10½/K	N
Metric (mm)	2.25	2.75	3.25	3.5	3.75	4.25	5	5.5	6	6.5	9.0

STITCH GUIDE

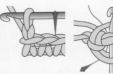

Need help? ▶ **StitchGuide.com** • ILLUSTRATED GUIDES • HOW-TO VIDEOS

STITCH ABBREVIATIONS

beg	begin/begins/beginning
bpdc	back post double crochet
bpsc	back post single crochet
bptr	back post treble crochet
CC	contrasting color
ch(s)	chain(s)
ch-	refers to chain or space previously made (i.e., ch-1 space)
ch sp(s)	chain space(s)
cl(s)	cluster(s)
cm	centimeter(s)
dc	double crochet (singular/plural)
dc dec	double crochet 2 or more stitches together, as indicated
dec	decrease/decreases/decreasing
dtr	double treble crochet
ext	extended
fpdc	front post double crochet
fpsc	front post single crochet
fptr	front post treble crochet
g	gram(s)
hdc	half double crochet
hdc dec	half double crochet 2 or more stitches together, as indicated
inc	increase/increases/increasing
lp(s)	loop(s)
MC	main color
mm	millimeter(s)
oz	ounce(s)
pc	popcorn(s)
rem	remain/remains/remaining
rep(s)	repeat(s)
rnd(s)	round(s)
RS	right side
sc	single crochet (singular/plural)
sc dec	single crochet 2 or more stitches together, as indicated
sk	skip/skipped/skipping
sl st(s)	slip stitch(es)
sp(s)	space(s)/spaced
st(s)	stitch(es)
tog	together
tr	treble crochet
trtr	triple treble
WS	wrong side
yd(s)	yard(s)
yo	yarn over

YARN CONVERSION

OUNCES TO GRAMS		GRAMS TO OUNCES	
1	28.4	25	7/8
2	56.7	40	1 2/3
3	85.0	50	1 3/4
4	113.4	100	3 1/2

UNITED STATES		UNITED KINGDOM
sl st (slip stitch)	=	sc (single crochet)
sc (single crochet)	=	dc (double crochet)
hdc (half double crochet)	=	htr (half treble crochet)
dc (double crochet)	=	tr (treble crochet)
tr (treble crochet)	=	dtr (double treble crochet)
dtr (double treble crochet)	=	ttr (triple treble crochet)
skip	=	miss

Single crochet decrease (sc dec): (Insert hook, yo, draw lp through) in each of the sts indicated, yo, draw through all lps on hook.

Example of 2-sc dec

Half double crochet decrease (hdc dec): (Yo, insert hook, yo, draw lp through) in each of the sts indicated, yo, draw through all lps on hook.

Example of 2-hdc dec

Reverse single crochet (reverse sc): Ch 1, sk first st, working from left to right, insert hook in next st from front to back, draw up lp on hook, yo and draw through both lps on hook.

Chain (ch): Yo, pull through lp on hook.

Single crochet (sc): Insert hook in st, yo, pull through st, yo, pull through both lps on hook.

Double crochet (dc): Yo, insert hook in st, yo, pull through st, [yo, pull through 2 lps] twice.

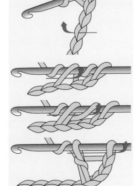

Double crochet decrease (dc dec): (Yo, insert hook, yo, draw lp through, yo, draw through 2 lps on hook) in each of the sts indicated, yo, draw through all lps on hook.

Example of 2-dc dec

Front loop (front lp) Back loop (back lp)

Front Loop   Back Loop

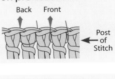

Front post stitch (fp): Back post stitch (bp): When working post st, insert hook from right to left around post of st on previous row.

Back   Front

← Post of Stitch

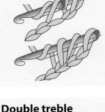

Half double crochet (hdc): Yo, insert hook in st, yo, pull through st, yo, pull through all 3 lps on hook.

Double treble crochet (dtr): Yo 3 times, insert hook in st, yo, pull through st, [yo, pull through 2 lps] 4 times.

Treble crochet decrease (tr dec): Holding back last lp of each st, tr in each of the sts indicated, yo, pull through all lps on hook.

Example of 2-tr dec

Slip stitch (sl st): Insert hook in st, pull through both lps on hook.

Chain color change (ch color change) Yo with new color, draw through last lp on hook.

Double crochet color change (dc color change) Drop first color, yo with new color, draw through last 2 lps of st.

Treble crochet (tr): Yo twice, insert hook in st, yo, pull through st, [yo, pull through 2 lps] 3 times.

101 Crochet Squares is published by Annie's, 306 East Parr Road, Berne, IN 46711. Printed in USA. Copyright © 2016 Annie's. All rights reserved. This publication may not be reproduced in part or in whole without written permission from the publisher.

RETAIL STORES: If you would like to carry this publication or any other Annie's publication, visit AnniesWSL.com.

Every effort has been made to ensure that the instructions in this publication are complete and accurate. We cannot, however, take responsibility for human error, typographical mistakes or variations in individual work. Please visit AnniesCustomerService.com to check for pattern updates.

ISBN: 978-1-59012-648-6   Library of Congress Control Number: 2016950342   1 2 3 4 5 6 7 8 9